Y0-BWG-828

KATIMA ... WHAT?

BY THE SAME AUTHOR

I Accuse the Assassins of Coffin, Éditions du Jour, 1964.

The Temple on the River, Harvest House, 1967.

Two Innocents in Red China (co-written with Pierre Elliott Trudeau), Oxford University Press, 1968.

The World is Round, McClelland & Stewart, 1976.

Have Them Build a Tower Together, McClelland & Stewart, 1979.

The Great Building-Bee (co-written with Maurice-F. Strong), General Publishing, 1980.

The Coffin Affair, General Publishing, 1981.

21 Days—One Man's Fight for Canada's Youth, Optimum Publishing, 1986.

Travelling in Tropical Countries, Hurtig Publishers, 1986.

Yemen—An Invitation to a Voyage in Arabia Felix, Heritage Publishing, 1989.

Hello, World!, Robert Davies Publishing – Talon Books, translated by Jean-Paul Murray 1996.

IN FRENCH

Autour des trois Amériques, Beauchemin, 1948. Fides 1952.

Autour de l'Afrique, Fides, 1950.

Aïcha l'Africaine, contes, Fides, 1950.

Aventures autour du monde, Fides, 1952.

Nouvelle aventure en Afrique, Fides, 1953.

Coffin était innocent, Éditions de l'Homme, 1958.

Scandale à Bordeaux, Éditions de l'Homme, 1959.

Deux innocents en Chine rouge (en collaboration avec Pierre Elliott Trudeau), Éditions de l'Homme, 1960.

J'accuse les assassins de Coffin, Éditions du Jour, 1963.

Trois jours en prison, Club du Livre du Québec, 1965.

Les Écœurants, Éditions du Jour, 1966. Stanké, 1987

Ah ! mes aïeux !, Éditions du Jour, 1968.

Obscénité et Liberté, Éditions du Jour, 1970.

Blablabla du bout du monde, Éditions du Jour, 1971.

La terre est ronde, Fides, 1976.

Faites-leur bâtir une tour ensemble, Éditions Héritage, 1979.

L'Affaire Coffin, Domino, 1980.

Le Grand Branle-bas (en collaboration avec Maurice-F. Strong). Les Quinze, 1980.

La Jeunesse des années 80 : état d'urgence, Éditions Héritage, 1982.

Voyager en pays tropical, Boréal Express, 1984.

Trois semaines dans le hall du Sénat, Éditions de l'Homme, 1986.

Yémen – Invitation au voyage en Arabie heureuse, Éditions Héritage, 1989.

Deux innocents dans un igloo, Héritage Jeunesse, 1990.

Deux innocents au Mexique, Héritage Jeunesse, 1990.

Deux innocents au Guatemala, Héritage Jeunesse, 1990.

Deux innocents en Amérique centrale, Héritage Jeunesse, 1991.

Bonjour, le monde !, Éditions Robert Davies, 1996.

Duplessis, non merci !, Éditions du Boréal, 2000.

IN GERMAN

Jemen – Einladung zu einer Reise nach Arabia felix, Azal Publishing, 1989.

Jacques Hébert

Translated by Jean-Paul Murray

KATIMA ... WHAT?

Twenty-five Thousand Kilometres
Along the Roads of Canada,
Visiting with the School of Life

Illustrated with 142 Photos and Video Stills
by Anthony Loring

C O S M O P O L I T E

Royalties coming from the sale of this book will be entirely donated to Katimavik.

Layout and cover design:
JOEL SKOGMAN + ANTHONY LORING

Copyright © 2001, COSMOPOLITE COMMUNICATIONS
Translation copyright © 2001, JEAN-PAUL MURRAY

ISBN : 2-9807262-1-4

Legal Deposit: National Library of Canada, 2001
                Bibliothèque national du Québec, 2001

DISTRIBUTION

English language edition:

GENERAL DISTRIBUTION SERVICES Ltd.
325, Humber College Blvd., Toronto, Ontario, Canada M9W 7C3
Tel.: (416) 312-1919
Fax: (416) 213-1917
Email: cservice@genpub.com

French language edition (KATIMA...QUOI?)

DIMÉDIA
539, Lebeau Blvd, Saint-Laurent, Québec, Canada H4N 1S2
Tel. : (514) 336-3941
Fax : (514) 331-3916
Email: commandes@dimedia.qc.ca

ÉDITEUR

COSMOPOLITE COMMUNICATIONS
C.P. 212, Succursale Victoria, Westmount, Québec, Canada H3Z 2V5

Acknowledgements

Although the purpose of the trip by Jacques Hébert and Anthony Loring was to promote Katimavik, the organization was in no position to fund it. Such an extravagance wasn't part of Katimavik's budget, so we had to rely on the generosity of a few friends who provided the money and equipment needed to complete the project.

Katimavik is profoundly indebted to these kind-hearted people without whom this trip, this book and the videos by Anthony Loring would have never existed. The following is a list of contributors in alphabetical order:

Angers, Philippe

Antoft, Kell

Bell Mobility

Clément, Jacques

Le Groupe Caron et Ménard Ltée

MacDougall, Reford

Frenette, Claude

Goodridge, Edythe

Rodriguez, Pablo

Saint-Germain, Robert

Smith, Michael D.

Zellers Family Foundation

TO THE HONOURABLE BARNETT DANSON, PC, OC

The first minister responsible for Katimavik,
an organization he was passionate about.

CONTENTS

CANADA

PREAMBLE

Why the devil set out on such a long trip through Canada, from Saint John's, Newfoundland, to the Yukon, in a van rigged out for camping, but whose comfort is relative? I thought I knew my country quite well, a land that's vast, immense, nearly as large as Europe. I've criss-crossed it back and forth since my teens, alas, mostly by train and airplane. Perhaps the only thing left for me was to drive across it, to drink in its miraculous, amazing, scenery, day after day, for three months ...

Let's say it right off: *never* would I've undertaken this long trip, at 77 years of age, without a powerful motive. It came to me by accident during a meeting with Katimavik participants in Vancouver.

One of them, looking rather strange with his shaggy lime-green coloured hair, tells me his story, summarised here from memory:

"Where are you from," I asked bluntly, to prompt the conversation.

"From Quebec City," he answered in French.

"The city itself?"

"Well, more or less ... "

"Which means?"

The 18 year old boy, with the lime-green mop, hesitates for a moment. Then, with an awkward smile:

"I'd been living on the street for two years. In Quebec City and the suburbs ... They call us street people. It's an infernal life. I really didn't know how I could get out of it.

One day, my mother, who lives on the North Shore, sent me a newspaper clipping: a thing called Katimavik was inviting young people aged 17 to 21 to participate in a seven-month program. I'd discover three regions of my country, learn English and various work skills, make friends ... I couldn't believe it. They'd never accept me! Someone without even a home, who dropped out of school ages ago ... "

"But you sent the application anyway ... "

"Well, I had nothing to lose! Except the cost of a stamp! I'd forgotten all about it when I got a letter from the Katimavik office telling me I'd been accepted as a participant. Wow! I couldn't believe my eyes! Wow! I reread the letter five times! My life would change overnight. And I couldn't begin to suspect how much! For the moment, what counted most was that I'd no longer be a 'street kid.' For the first time in two years, I'd have a roof over my head, that of a Katimavik house, where I'd join ten other young people from every corner of Canada. I could count on three meals a day. But, cooler yet, I had ten new friends whom I considered as brothers and sisters, and with whom I'd share seven months of terrific experiences."

"Such as?"

"I'd never travelled. And now I was going to live and work in three different provinces: in Quebec, in Saint-Joachim-de-Courval, in East Vancouver, British Columbia, where we are now, and soon, in Goderich, Ontario, on the shores of Lake Huron. At first, I didn't know a word of English. I now consider myself bilingual. Wow! My numerous work experiences have given me all kinds of ideas for the future. One thing's absolutely sure: I'll never again be a street kid. Thank you, Katimavik!"

A beautiful moving story I must've told a hundred times since ... But the guy with the lime-green hair still has a word to say:

"There's this other street kid my age who sent an application. He wasn't as lucky: his application was turned down due to a lack of space. It's not fair! He might've escaped the street as well, and found a better life."

"You're right: it's not fair!"

We say farewell on that note, and I return to Montreal, the biting conclusion of a young participant met by chance ringing in my head: "It's not fair!"

In fact, Katimavik wasn't created for the sole purpose of pulling Quebec City street kids from their hellish condition, but to wrench the greatest number of young Canadians from a life that's lousy, selfish, closed to the world, whether they're sons of the bourgeoisie, or daughters of the unemployed, students lost in the absurd mazes of our education system, or dropouts in the midst of despair, young people who still have ideals, or apprentice drug addicts who no longer believe in anything.

In the plane carrying me back from Vancouver, I ask my friend Jean-Guy Bigeau, Katimavik's Executive Director, how many candidates he'll again have to turn down this year, due to an inadequate budget: "More than 4,000 ... "[1] he answers somewhat apologetically, as though this were his fault.

---

1   *In 1999 and 2000, Katimavik accepted 1,587 young people and turned away 9,079.*

Makes for a lot of "assassinated Mozarts," as Saint-Éxupéry would say. Apart from a few suicides for statistical purposes, these thousands of young people will manage to survive as best they can, but many will waste their lives amid pervading mediocrity, the pettiness of consumer society, with some, alas, falling into delinquency. Because Katimavik turned them away!

While our governments don't hesitate to sink billions of dollars into fighting unemployment, drugs, alcohol, dropping out, delinquency, they're totally stingy with their millions when it comes to investing in those rare programs able to give hope to young people and make them citizens that are more dynamic, self-sufficient, open, fraternal, free of prejudice, empowered in their turn to profoundly change our society.

"It's not fair!" The cry of my green-haired dishevelled young friend ceaselessly haunts me like a criticism and condemnation. If, after over twenty years of efforts we haven't yet been able to convince governments that Katimavik is the bargain of the century and that all young Canadians so wishing should be given access to it (like we all have access to health care!), it's likely because we haven't used the right arguments: *mea culpa!*

Till now, governments had used the excuse that financial problems and deficits meant they had to reduce to a minimum their investments in the noblest causes, youth for example. This is no longer the case.

Meanwhile, Katimavik's budget remains so low that we'll turn away 6,400 young people in 2001. Katimavik, which has proven itself after two decades of conclusive achievements, as evidenced by 21,000 former participants, their families, friends. Katimavik, which enjoys an international reputation, having earned a United Nations award, which has directly inspired similar programs in Australia, California, New York, etc. Katimavik, which has left its mark in some 1,780 Canadian communities, not only in concrete terms (the creation of parks, buildings, ecological trails; various initiatives designed to improve quality of life and the environment), but also in the area of human relations by putting these communities into contact with young people from every region in the country and vice versa.

But then, why don't governments ever come and beg Katimavik to offer its program, not to 957^2 young people a year, but to 5,000, 10,000, 20,000?

A deep mystery to me. And I'm not blaming anyone save myself perhaps for not succeeding, after nearly a quarter century, in making all political men and women from every party aware of Katimavik, as well as all levels of government, all bureaucrats (something already more difficult!) and even the media, who are sympathetic to Katimavik, but who don't talk about it every day by virtue of the principle that "good news is no news!"

That's when I got the idea for this lengthy road trip (25,000 kilometres) through all Canadian provinces, the Northwest Territories and the Yukon. The objective: promoting Katimavik by every means possible, through meetings with

---

2 *This figure for 2001 includes the 81 project leaders, who are also young people.*

the 38 groups spread from coast to coast, with communities, mayors, municipal councillors, members of Parliament and provincial Assemblies, senators and other notables, without forgetting television, radio and newspaper interviews. In short, to make people discover Katimavik, the School of Life!

Naturally, I couldn't imagine what the short- and long-term repercussions of such a trip would be. I only knew from experience that more things happen when you move than when you stay still!

Having travelled somewhat in my youth over the roads of Africa, Asia and Latin America, I knew the most practical and economical means of transportation would be a van equipped for camping. I also needed a good travelling companion. And, finally, state-of-the-art equipment to increase the enterprise's repercussions: computer, cell phones, camcorder, digital camera, etc.

All this would be costly, and the money would obviously have to be found outside Katimavik's budget. You can imagine the scandal: "Katimavik's founding president is having the government pay for his three-month vacation through Canada. And yackety-yack … "

We therefore brought together a small group of friends who were, like me, convinced that the trip would benefit Katimavik and, as a result, the youth of our country.

From one meeting to the next, we found new supporters: the van would be loaned to us for three months, as would the computer, telephones, video and digital cameras, etc. But we also needed cash for gas, food, ferries, campgrounds, etc. Thanks to a few generous friends, we soon found the thousands of necessary dollars.³

The question of the travelling companion remained. From experience, I knew it was crucial ...

I needed a volunteer, no salary having been provided for by the budget. My first idea: to find, with help from Katimavik's five regional offices, five volunteers who'd accompany me during the visit to their region of the country. Each would give three weeks to the cause, which is more reasonable than three months.

I secretly told myself that if one of these five volunteers proved a bad driver, poor photographer or a drag, the ordeal wouldn't last as long!

In June, a few weeks before leaving Montreal for Saint John's, where, naturally, the "official" departure ceremony would take place, I contacted Rachel Robichaud, Katimavik's project coordinator in Nova Scotia. I asked her to suggest, from among former participants or project leaders in her region, a travelling companion (bilingual assistant, guide, driver, photographer, videographer, etc.) ready to share my joys and sorrows in the four Atlantic provinces, for about three weeks. *Gratis pro Deo!*

A short while later, Rachel suggests one of her project leaders, available from the end of June: Anthony Loring. She speaks of him with such warmth that I anticipate Anthony's phone call with some curiosity.

Deep voice. Very serious. Too much so? We'd see. Modest: when I ask whether he's comfortable with all my

---

3 See Acknowledgements, page 7.

electronic and audiovisual hardware, he answers simply: "Yes." Later, once on the road, I understood that computers, videos and other cameras held no secret for him: he'd studied three years at Concordia University in those areas.

I ask him a few harmless questions:

"Do you have a sense of humour?"

Very seriously, Anthony answers:

"Yes."

"You'll need it!"

Suddenly, after I'd suggested I might consider travelling through the Atlantic provinces with him, he tells me in his most serious tone:

"I'd rather do the *whole* trip with you … "

"Through all of Canada? For three months? With no salary?

"Right."

I feel cornered. If I accept this extremely generous offer, I'll live for nearly three months with this young man I know absolutely nothing about, except that he's been a very good project leader over the last months.

What if he turned out to be a terrible driver, or a boozer? What if his sense of humour wasn't as obvious as he alleges?

Before answering, I chat a little more, learning that he'd participated in Canada World Youth in Brazil when he was 18 years old. He even claims I met him during an "official" visit to that country in 1989, and that I spoke to him briefly... as I did with the twenty or thirty other participants! Unfortunately, I have no recollection of the 18 year-old Anthony, but this anecdote reassures me somewhat: we have a few things in common...

What impresses me even more is his generosity: without hesitation, this 28 year-old man is offering three months of his life to Katimavik. Naturally, he'll discover corners of Canada for himself, but in conditions that aren't always easy, following an itinerary that will surely avoid Niagara Falls and make crazy detours to see a Katimavik group in some tiny remote village. In the company of an "old" man, a 77 year-old who could be his grandfather!

"Three months! A huge risk ..."

"For both of us!" he concludes, laughing.

At the end of this phone conversation we'd reached an agreement. For better or worse!

* * *

In the course of this account, illustrated by Anthony's photos, I'll draw abundantly from my travel diary, written each night without exception. On occasion, I'll quote one of the hundreds of participants met between Newfoundland and the Yukon; this will be even easier since they were interviewed by Anthony who, along the way, to top it all off, recorded the videos Katimavik urgently needed.

Have a nice trip!

Chapter 1

THE FALSE START

From Quebec to Newfoundland

June 22, 2000

I turned 77 yesterday. So long Tintin!

Anthony awaits me in Cap-Pelé, New Brunswick, where a debriefing of the project leaders from his Katimavik team is taking place. So I'll leave Montreal with another travelling companion, Alain Choinière, with whom I've been preparing the trip for the last several weeks. He'll be responsible for the journey's logistics: contacts with Katimavik's regional offices, with coordinators, project leaders, former participants, Friends of Katimavik, the media, etc.

The van has been outfitted as a camper[4] and impresses us right away: it handles well, has reasonable gas mileage, and offers space well designed for cooking, eating, writing and sleeping. Given my advanced age, I'll sleep on a good mattress at ground level, while my assistant gets the upper berth: a kind of tent pops up when the vehicle's roof is raised, providing a bunk of stretched canvas.

Today, we scurry nonstop to Pointe-à-la-Garde, where two old friends of Katimavik, Denise and Jacques Clément, await us for dinner. They're vacationing on the sunny shores of the Baie des Chaleurs. The family's been invited, and it's a feast: a sublime seafood gratin, washed down with plenty of white wine.

I inaugurate my bed in the camper which, in French, we'll

quite simply call the *van*, an anglicism included in the *Petit Robert* dictionary to designate "a vehicle used to transport race horses." Oh well! As long as we admit it's an anglicism, we're nearly forgiven!

Naturally, the Cléments had prepared two guest rooms for us. Thank you, but I prefer sleeping "at home," as I will throughout the journey. Alain, however, isn't too keen on the "tent" perched atop the vehicle, opting instead for the bourgeois luxury of the small guest cottage. But virtue is always rewarded: I slept like a log, while my unfortunate companion was devoured by mosquitoes all night!

June 23

Up at 6:00 a.m. Breakfast with our friends and, at 8:30, we set out for New Brunswick and Cap-Pelé, with its disturbing name (in French, *pelé* means either mangy or bald), but which is in fact a quaint Acadian village by the ocean, in this case the Strait of Northumberland, across from Prince Edward Island.

Meeting in a cottage rented for the debriefing are the project leaders, their coordinator, Rachel Robichaud, and staff from the Atlantic regional office. I finally meet Anthony, whom I vaguely know thanks to three brief phone calls: bearded, muscular, serious, good sense of humour. That should do!

A dinner of seafood and good cheer. Anthony's colleagues revel in asking us embarrassing questions, arguing that they're making sure we're compatible and that this trip by two people separated by a half century doesn't turn into a disaster. We pass the test, more or less …

June 24

Brunch at the Cap-Pelé Katimavik house with a group of participants and a few notables, including the member of the legislative Assembly and the member of Parliament.

It so happens this isn't the regular seven-month program

In Cap-Pelé, with Anthony's colleagues. (Photo Alain Choinière)

(which is already too brief, alas!) but an experimental nine-week project called LeaderPlus designed for young people aged between 22 and 26. Too many necessary elements are lacking for this abridged program to be compared with the regular one, but it will be useful if it prepares leaders and, among others, project leaders for Katimavik.

The Honourable Joe Landry, a former Senate colleague, joins us to share a birthday cake. In a group of eleven participants, it's always someone's birthday! The former senator is a lobster magnate in the region and offers us a large bagful of the crustaceans so the group can enjoy a treat tonight. Meanwhile, we treat ourselves with pancakes,

Participants in Cap-Pelé, N.B. (Photo Alain Choinière)

omelettes, brioches and pastries prepared by participants.

I play the innocent: "This bread's excellent. Did you buy it in Cap-Pelé?"

Our two politicians in turn praise the good whole-wheat bread, which mustn't be lacking in fibre. Participants laugh: they prepared everything themselves, including the bread, a masterpiece signed Chris Sampson, a guy from Labrador. Among a thousand other things, participants all learn to knead bread dough. If all politicians had the opportunity to eat pancakes with a group of participants and taste Chris Sampson's bread, Katimavik would no longer have any problems!

June 25

Farewells to Alain: like a big boy, he'll take the train back to Montreal.

Departure from Cap-Pelé with Anthony, still somewhat stunned by the reality which suddenly strikes him. By climbing into our brand new vehicle, he must be thinking, as I do, that this sheet-metal box will be our house, office and means of transportation over the next months.

Our immediate objective: reaching Newfoundland in forty-eight hours. We cautiously get to know each other, while admiring the lovely landscape of New Brunswick and Nova Scotia.

At lunch time, somewhere on Cape Breton, we stop in the shade of large maples. Through their bright green foliage, we glimpse the glimmering of Bras d'Or Lake, a strip of the Atlantic splashing the island's whole interior.

First meal on the road, with perhaps 250 more to go ... We'd already resolved to eat well, by avoiding fast food and restaurants which were, besides, beyond our means. The menu at noon: avocados in olive oil, tuna and tomato sand-wiches, made with whole-wheat bread—needless to say—soya milk and bananas.

First night in a public campground near North Sydney, where we'll take the ferry tomorrow morning for the small port of Argentia. An old farm with an unobstructed view of the glistening Bras d'Or Lake.

Chapter 2

THE REAL START

Newfoundland

June 26

Up at 5:30 a.m. to make sure we don't miss the M.V. Joseph and Clara Smallwood, an imposing ferry that will take us to Newfoundland ... in a mere fifteen hours!

We take advantage of this break to put our notes and accounts in order, while assessing the possibilities of our impressive electronic and audiovisual arsenal, which remains a complete mystery to me. Thank God, Anthony seems perfectly familiar with all these wonderful gadgets. Or else fakes it very convincingly!

Since we're unable to cook, we make do with the cafeteria, definitely not the Mecca of Newfoundland gastronomy. Montignac would surely faint: slimy pizzas, greasy hamburgers (heroically translated as *hambourgeois*, because things are done bilingually on board!), with everything drowned in a thick brownish sauce, the same one found on the chicken, fish, pork chops, and even the French fries already swimming in cholesterol.

But Newfoundlanders are so nice they'd make us swallow anything ... with help from a good sip of screech!

I read, write and sleep while Anthony explores the ship and takes in the Atlantic, which he's sailing for the first time.

The sky is gray, the ocean is gray, everything is gray aboard this functional ship which is no shiny Love Boat ...

We dock around 11:00 p.m. at the port of Argentia, then drive through the night along a small winding road which, as we'd find out the next day, is somewhat hazardous because of the moose brazenly haunting it.

Following a wrong turn and several detours, we return almost to our starting point, ending up in a park near Argentia. We spend the night there, in the middle of a dark and shivery pine grove.

June 27

At 6:00 a.m. we head straight north, avoiding Saint John's: we're expected first at Terra Nova National Park, where Katimavik groups have worked hard over the last two years.

Notified by Alain thanks to the cell phone, we stop in Clarenceville to give our regards to Sheila Kelly Blackmore, who'd been a project leader in the eighties. After devoting twenty-odd years to others, she recently began running a large motel where she's invited us for lunch. It would be hard to miss it: a large bright billboard greets us and, on the poles in front of her establishment, Sheila has had the Katimavik flag raised beside that of Newfoundland and Canada. She's even summoned the local press: first interview of the trip!

Very good roads to Terra Nova Park. In front of the administrative building, standing in the heavy wind, Edythe

The Katimavik flag against the Newfoundland sky.

Goodridge awaits us. She's an old friend who remains young: she's had a passion for Katimavik ever since she was a board member. In the "good old days"...

When I called her barely two months ago, asking her to revive the Friends of Katimavik group, she agreed with her characteristic generosity and boundless joy.

We fall into each other's arms, refusing to believe our last meeting was a decade ago.

Park officials have organized a small reception to express their gratitude to Katimavik, whose participants worked very hard in the woods around here over the last two years. Another group was expected this year but, due to a lack of funds, Katimavik resigned itself to not having a project in Newfoundland before next year. "It's not fair," as they say.

Guests include the Honourable Fred Mifflin, the local MP and a former minister. The following are a few shreds of the powerful speech he gave:

"Katimavik is without question the finest youth program Canada ever had …"

Hurrah! It's good to here this now and again!

"The presence and work of its participants, from every corner of Canada, has contributed to the development of this region and, especially, of *my* park," he insists, smiling.

"It's unfortunate that Katimavik can't expand and that it's absent from Newfoundland this year. But Jacques Hébert knows he can count on my support in Ottawa …"

I get acquainted with Valérie Poirier-Payette, a Quebec participant who finished her work experience in the park on April 12. She liked the experience so much she'll continue working here until the fall, then return to her province to pursue her studies. Valérie introduces me to her host family, with whom she lived for two weeks, as is standard practice. She'll now live with them until September.

Farewell to all these wonderful people. Edythe Goodridge, who lives nearby, will join us in Saint John's tomorrow.

In the evening, we have no trouble finding a campground: a superb one is located in the park. Someone at the gate tells us we're guests of the house: our small patch of forest won't cost a thing!

June 28

On the road to Saint John's: 240 kilometres, a few hours. More happy reunions: Bruce Gilbert, a project leader in the eighties, now executive director of the Newfoundland

Valerie Poirier-Payette on right, with host family.

Conservation Corps, "largely inspired by Katimavik," he says, with a complicitous smile.

Along with Edythe, Bruce is one of the driving forces behind the Friends of Katimavik in Newfoundland and, naturally, of the small celebration organized for the so-called "official" departure, in presence of the province's premier, the Honourable Brian Tobin.

We have countless memories in common and Bruce reminds me of a few:

"Do you remember when we met in Saint John's, Newfoundland, with Brian Arsenault, who was in charge of the region at the time?"

How could I forget! January 29, 1986, Canada's Secretary of State, the Honourable Benoît Bouchard, announced what he believed to be Katimavik's death sentence: the government was cutting all funding! In an ultimate effort to convince the government to change its decision, I set out on a media tour that took me to Vancouver, Edmonton, Regina, Winnipeg, Toronto, Montreal, Quebec City, Halifax, Fredericton, Charlottetown, and, finally, to Saint John's.

Accompanied by Brian Arsenault and Bruce Gilbert, in the small lobby of the NTV station in Saint John's, I tried to assess not only the impact of this media blitz but, especially, of the efforts of the Friends of Katimavik which had sprouted throughout the country. Thanks to them, newspapers, members of Parliament and Prime Minister Mulroney got hundreds of letters. They also gathered tens of thousands of signatures on petitions that were then tabled in the House of Commons by Liberal and New Democratic opposition members.

Brian, Bruce and I agreed on one point: I'd really used *all* the regular means of pressuring public opinion and the government.

That's where we were in our musings, when Brian Arsenault blurted out, jokingly:

"A hunger strike is all you have left!"

After bursting with laughter, I suddenly began thinking out loud about this strange idea. When I left my friends to head back to Montreal, my decision had been taken.[5]

That's the incident Bruce reminded me of, nearly fifteen years later …

Meeting with Bruce Gilbert in St-John's, Nfld.

Lunch at the Ship Inn, a quaint little restaurant where we meet our dear Edythe, as well as Bob Stone, another strong advocate we've been told a great deal about: he chaired the Local Katimavik Committee on Bell Island, a lovely little island of 2,500 inhabitants, located in Conception Bay, facing Saint John's. For the last three years, Bob has devoted himself to ensuring Katimavik's success on his island. He insists on taking us there tomorrow, following the ceremony, to meet, for lack of partici-

5   *21 Days—One Man's Struggle for Canada's Youth, Optimum Publishing, 1986.*

pants, a few individuals nostalgic for Katimavik: partners, work supervisors, host families, etc.

Meanwhile, everyone insists that Anthony not leave the island before going to Signal Hill, an extremely historic spot overlooking the narrow entrance to the Port of Saint John's. Conscientiously, I accompany him but, as is often the case, the bay is covered in fog. So there's nothing to see save for, naturally, a few rusty cannons recalling the battles between the British and French for control of the island (and the cod!). In 1762, the British got the last word. More recently, in 1901, it's again here that Marconi received the first words transmitted across the Atlantic by wireless telegraph. Though Anthony may not have seen a thing, he'll be able to add a few dates to his culture!

Oh! The pleasure of learning that Saint John's is one of the rare cities having a large wild park within municipal boundaries. With a campground boasting 185 sites. We'll therefore camp at Pippy Park, a stone's throw from downtown.

June 29

At about 11:00 a.m., numerous Friends of Katimavik gather at the Resource Centre for the Arts, a cultural centre recently renovated with help from Katimavik participants. An ideal point of departure ...

Barely a few weeks previously, I'd phoned the Premier of Newfoundland and Labrador, the Honourable Brian Tobin, inviting him to preside over this event. He hadn't hesitated for a second:

"You know I've always supported Katimavik. So I'm delighted and proud to help you promote it somewhat."

Needless to say the presence of the young and dynamic premier ensures that of all the media.

The Honourable Brian Tobin, Premier of Newfoundland, at the departure ceremony.

Edythe Goodridge and I welcome this warmhearted and genuine man. Contrary to so many of the politicians I've met, he *really* listens to his counterpart and is interested in what's being said to him. His words are spoken from the heart, not from notes prepared by assistants.

Brian Tobin therefore wings a brief and hard-hitting speech, broadcast by all the province's media … if only it had been heard across the country!

He recalls the years when Katimavik disappeared, its discrete return ... which should be less so now that the federal government is enjoying large surpluses!

"In Canada, today, we too frequently speak to each other through megaphones! We address each other as though we were Monopoly players ... And, more often than not, we talk about what divides us rather than about what unites us. We're still a small population spread out over a huge country, and we still need to get to know each other, and to live with each other and support each other."

The premier mentions benefits valued at some $75 million[6] provided by Katimavik in thousands of work experiences throughout Canada:

"Your young people go to live in communities, are paid only a few dollars a day, giving of themselves heart and soul to improve life in those communities, far from their homes, somewhere in this country. What better way for Canadians to get to know each other? And, in particular, for young Canadians to get to know their country?"

Thanking him, I recall his courageous stand in 1986, when the federal government of the day had sounded Katimavik's death knell. As an opposition member of Parliament, he'd tabled petitions in the House of Commons signed by thousands of Newfoundlanders supporting Katimavik and the hunger strike.

Spontaneous testimonies follow from several people in the audience, all of them somehow related to Katimavik: former participants, project leaders, coordinators, host fami-

---

6   *Calculated according to the average salary paid in the community sector.*

lies, board members, partners, etc. We should quote them all, but, out of principle, we'll only single out the testimonies of former participants: Wendy Ross, a pioneer from 1977, the first year of the program, and Phil Smith, who's just barely completed the 1999-2000 program.

According to Wendy, Katimavik is what helped her find her vocation as an archeologist:

"The last three months of the program took place in Dawson City, Yukon. I discovered archeology as a result of the volunteer work assigned to me. When I returned to Newfoundland, I registered at Memorial University, where I obtained a degree in archeology. Today, I work as an archeologist here, in Saint John's. I've never stopped being interested in Katimavik and, again this year, I chaired the Local Katimavik Committee, etc."

Wendy Ross, a Newfoundland archeologist and participant in 1977.

And then a tall young man with an intense gaze stands up: Phil Smith from Summerside, Newfoundland. He's just completed the program ... Twenty-two years after Wendy! He begins by admitting that, before Katimavik, he was very shy and seriously lacked confidence: it's hardly believable when seeing the ease with which he testifies before the media and a sizeable audience, which includes the premier of his province:

"Katimavik is one of the greatest things that ever happened to me. At first, I had some personal problems, including a lack of confidence in my abilities: I've come out of the program a better person than ever! I've got friends for life: in my group, in my three host families, a little everywhere along the road. I phone many of them every week. We talk for hours ... as we did again last night! Katimavik is one of the greatest things I've ever experienced and, since my

Phil Smith from Summerside, Newfoundland, a participant in 2000.

return, I can't help but recommending it strongly to all the young people my age I meet. I wholeheartedly support those calling for extra funding …"

At least ten or so people stood to give often very moving testimonies. Brian Tobin listens to all this with very genuine interest since, at the end, he can't resist going back to the microphone to give another brief speech, even more rousing than the first one.

He was deeply moved by the testimonies he just heard and says so. Suddenly, he admits that, last night, for the first time, he listened to an episode of the series *Survivor.*

"Here are a group of people, brought together in challenging circumstances. They must build a team, while competing to survive, and ensure that only one person wins … after eliminating all the others!"

"And then I told myself that this situation really reflects our society which has gone adrift. You know, our communities have lost their sense of balance to a very large extent."

"We need Katimavik to remind us what communities are all about. We need to remember what it means to "support each other," and not be the last person standing, but to help those who have trouble standing become part of the community."

"We need to go back to the community values of which Katimavik is a living example."

The Honourable Tobin concludes with an appeal to his colleagues in Ottawa to restore Katimavik's funding to allow it to offer its program not to 1,000, but to at least 5,000 young Canadians.

As was fitting, Edythe Goodridge got the last word . . . The trip can begin!

In the afternoon, as promised, we follow Bob Stone, who's absolutely delighted to show us Bell Island where, over the last three years, nine Katimavik groups spent particularly happy and productive days.

Judging from the ferry captain's warm greeting, partici-pants have left their mark in the area. He bluntly refuses to let us pay for the crossing: "Katimavik participants have crossed free of charge for the last three years, as often as they wanted. They deserved it, considering all the work they did on the island!"

Brian Tobin returning to the microphone!

Edythe Goodridge gets the last word…

Chairman of the Local Katimavik Committee, Bob Stone has acted as a link between participants and the fourteen work partners. An unpretentious man with a huge heart. He's barely 40 years-old but, due to a serious work accident, was forced into early retirement … which his tireless activity for Katimavik has literally filled and delighted.

Bob is really proud to have us for dinner in his modest house, located at the centre of Bell Island. While the soup simmers, he shows us his "family albums," filled with photos of the hundreds of participants who've lived and worked on the island since 1997. He knows them all by name, describes their character, their habits even, as though they were his own children.

"This is Benoît, a guy from Quebec. A wonderful participant! He'll be in the Yukon, doing his third rotation, when you get there. Don't forget to tell him Bob says hi."

He also mentions William, another Quebec participant who's made a strong impression on him:

"One day, as we were walking, he suddenly told me: 'Bob, walk a little more slowly!' 'But why?' I asked. 'To take the time to appreciate the great beauty of Bell Island, your island ...' "

"Until then, it had never even occurred to me that Bell Island could be beautiful. I'd never taken a good look at it before a young Quebecer named William told me to walk more slowly. Since that day, I look at and enjoy the scenery of my island. Without Katimavik, this probably would have never happened to me ..."

While Bob cooks away in his kitchen, we go over to set up our house atop a promontory overlooking magnificent scenery. Before us, a lighthouse displays its proud profile against a sea and a sky that are so blue: how right William was!

The cell phone doesn't stop ringing: Alain provides our instructions for the next few days, a journalist interviews us for the *National Post*, another for CBC's *Newsworld*, friends inquire about our health, a little worried, we're not too sure why.

Bob Stone, a pillar of Katimavik in Bell Island, Nfld.

June 30

This time, Bob has to walk faster than usual, because he's promised to give us a tour of *all* the institutions where Katimavik participants worked over the last three years.

A very demanding round taking us through an abandoned cemetery whose tombstones were uncovered and inscriptions re-transcribed, and an iron mine, abandoned as well, then restored as a tourist attraction. Then to the kindergarten school, the Boys and Girls Club, the library, the food bank, a greenhouse for the handicapped, a foot path, the highschool, all the places where Katimavik participants worked very hard, as those in charge are willing to testify: "Oh! Why don't you send us your boys and girls again this year?" What answer can I give?

At the end of the evening, we return to our campground, near Argentia.

Chapter 3

FIRST CONTACT WITH THE SCHOOL OF LIFE

Nova Scotia, Prince Edward Island,
New Brunswick

July 1

Up at 5:30 a.m. A trouble-free crossing aboard the M.V. Joseph and Clara Smallwood, though fog wraps us like a soft eiderdown right up to North Sydney, which we reach at 11:30 p.m. We return to our old Bras d'Or campground. We do have our little habits!

July 3

We drive to Bridgewater, Nova Scotia, where Kell Antoft and his wife await us in a beautiful log cottage on the edge of a lake. A former university professor, Kell is a pillar of Katimavik, a member of the board the year of the Great Disruption. When Katimavik rose from its ashes in 1994, he immediately returned to the board.

Since there are no groups in the area, we'll settle for visiting a recreation centre in Peace Time Park, where Katimavik had distinguished itself in the eighties. Its director, Carroll Randall, remembers our presence here very keenly: "Your participants did a lot of work, which the community benefits from to this day."

We stop in Halifax. Several interesting encounters, including one with Cynthia Martin, a Year 1 participant, whom I meet again ... after 22 years! One of the characters in my

With Kell Antoft, visiting a work site in Bridgewater, N.S.

book *Have Them Build a Tower Together*. She brought along her copy of the book, as if I could've forgotten such a strong and captivating personality!

Born in Toronto, Cynthia now lives in Halifax—more evidence that former Katimavik participants feel at home anywhere in Canada.

July 4

On the road to Amherst, where we'll spend the night with a group who are the very end of their seven-month program. We chat till midnight or almost ...

July 5

Appointment at city hall with Amherst mayor Jerry Hallee. A steadfast Katimavik supporter, he doesn't have to be persuaded. He invited present participants and several former ones to this meeting, and insists everyone sign the guest book.

We're running a little late and have to work twice as hard. We make a flying visit to another experimental Leader group (16 to 19 years of age), located in the world's most beautiful surroundings, in Tidnish, Nova Scotia.

Cynthia Martin, a moving chapter in "Have Them Build a Tower Together."

Another hasty visit with participants of the Leader group in Lockport ... they arrived only yesterday! Still suffering from jetlag! We share breakfast before the reception organized by the Local Katimavik Committee with the mayor and other friends, who've even come from the neighbouring municipality of Shelburne, where Katimavik has deep roots.

A dreamy setting in Tidnish, N.S.

July 5

Return to New Brunswick. In Memramcook, we get acquainted with a group of ten participants which has dubbed itself a "dream team." Guys and girls resplendent with health, intelligent, curious, with great attitudes, proud to have succeeded so well in the program that's about to end.

We occasionally meet groups who aren't as happy, just as in life there are families who aren't as blissful as others, but today's group is exceptional. We trade stories, solve the world's problems, laughing a great deal as well. Til midnight!

July 6

At 10:00 a.m., the municipality hosts a reception in what they call the "Monument" in these parts, a former academic hall of the old Saint Joseph's college. Memories ... In the fifties, when I returned from some trip to Africa or elsewhere, I'd come to relate my "exploits" to students at this college. A huge hall whose acoustics are so perfect you can speak to an audience of several hundred people without using a microphone. Following a recital here, Yehudi Menuhin declared that, till then, he'd never been able to draw such a tone from his Stradivarius. So delighted, that he declined his fee!

Breakfast with the group in Lockport-Shelburne, N.S

For lack of violin recitals, we listen to several speeches from the assembled notables: mayor, federal and provincial representatives, presidents of this or that, all unanimous in praising Katimavik. Out of sheer modesty, we won't quote anyone!

In Memramcook, N.B., with staff from the Atlantic office.

Another delightful moment of the day is the lunch with the team from the Atlantic regional office, Anthony's "bosses" over the last few months: Rachel Robichaud, Roch Poirier, Jacinthe Dufour and Dominique Lebrun.

It's hard to describe the mood of such an encounter ... Besides Anthony, I barely know the others. Yet, I have the strange impression I've known them forever, no doubt because we share a common passion, which is certainly a good reason to get along. We have very serious discussions but, especially, we laugh. For nearly two hours ...

I appreciate my luck in being so easily accepted, both at Katimavik and Canada World Youth, by all those young people, whose father or grandfather I could be. They're certainly more of a laugh than people my age, especially those who accept being old and who only ever talk about their blessed triple bypass or prostate problems.

Anthony's father, who lives in Riverview, right across from Moncton, invites us for lunch. He's delighted that, despite all our differences, we manage to get along: "You'll have a good trip!" he concludes.

Anthony and Jacques in front of their van. (Photo Jacinthe Dufour)

Nice pasta dish with tomatoes and fresh basil, "grown in this house," washed down with red wine. According to his commendable habit, Anthony never consumes a drop of alcohol if he is to drive our dear van.

Anthony's mother was unable to join us since she works in a Moncton hospital, so we drop in on her and relax over a coffee.

So here I am on the best of terms with the Loring family, which might help me understand the son, who never completely drops his guard.

Next stop, Abram Village, a small Acadian community on Prince Edward Island, where the Katimavik house shelters participants who, let's say, aren't as happy as those in Memramcook. There's even a little glumness in the air. (Something we'll observe nowhere else on this trip.)

I sit in midst of the group, in the common room: "So, tell me about your problems!"

Participants don't need to be coaxed. In one case, it's the fault of such a project leader who's incompetent, in

The Abram Village group, less jovial let's say...

another, that of a regional director interpreting conduct rules his own way and threatening to dismiss four participants who, furiously, decide to abandon the program immediately, leaving the others in complete disarray, etc.

Not knowing all the facts, I carefully avoid taking sides. But, this time, I can't help thinking that Katimavik may have flaws, that we'll have to investigate, and prevent a similar situation from recurring.

July 7

While I converse with our partners and the local press, Anthony continues discussing with participants. His group-leader instinct gets the best of him and he clamours unceremoniously: "Snap out of it! Stop feeling sorry for yourselves! You admit to liking Stephanie, your group leader. Well, stop making life miserable for her and for yourselves. You live in a good house, the weather is great, the ocean is beautiful, your work project is interesting, and there are nearly two months of summer left to save your program …"

An aggressive Quebec girl bawls out Anthony:

"You have no right to talk to us that way! You don't even know us!"

"That's right, I'm listening to you, trying to know you …"

"You don't know me!" cries out the raging participant.

Anthony then invites her for a stroll in the park. I don't know what they said to each other, but as we were about to leave, the participant looked Anthony right in the eye, saying only one word to him: "Thanks!"

After greeting us rather coldly last night, the group now flocks around us. Participants insist we accompany them back to the house, where they take out their cameras for the group pictures. Watch the birdie! Everyone smiles. Finally!

With the group in Abram Village, all smiles...

Well, we leave Abram Village rather proud of ourselves!

Return to Nova Scotia over the endless bridge now linking Prince Edward Island to the continent. I'm one of those nostalgic people, an enemy of progress, who miss the old ferry.

One day, when I was barely 16, it had carried me to this island at the ends of the earth to learn English.

During the two school years I spent on the island, besides learning English, I'd made a staggering discovery: there were people outside Quebec who resemble us like brothers, even though they speak another language and belong to another culture. That revelation had a profound effect on my life and, to the young journalist who earlier asked me why, how and where the idea for Katimavik came to me,

I was able to answer, without much exaggeration: "It was right here, on your island, at the small Saint Dunstan's College in Charlottetown. I was 16, etc."

We purchase strawberries by the roadside, the first of the season, absolute marvels. We savour them by the banks of Blue River, still under the shock of our difficult day in Abram Village ...

Chapter 4

FROM ONE RECTORY
TO THE OTHER
Quebec

July 8

Return to Quebec and arrival at Pohénégamook, whose name has always fascinated me … and which I still have trouble spelling! A spectacular village whose white houses fan out around the lake like a domino game.

We already know that the Katimavik house is empty: we arrive precisely when participants leave their group to live for two weeks, individually, with what we call "host families." A proven method for helping participants integrate into the community, for better understanding the local culture, and for some, immersing themselves in the "other language."

The Katimavik house in Pohénégamook.

We'll see the participants tomorrow morning, accompanied by their host families, during a brunch at the Outdoor Centre. We camp by the edge of the lake, beside their large empty house.

July 9

The Outdoor Centre is one of the places where participants lived and worked for hundreds of hours. This brunch
is a kind of celebration for them. Each introduces us to
their "mother," their "father," their "brothers," or their "sisters." We can already sense the wonderful relationship
between them.

Liam Pierce from Prince George, B.C., feels at home in Quebec.

Anthony grabs a participant at random and interviews him
on video: Liam Pierce, a boy from Prince George, British
Columbia, at the other end of the country. He takes the
learning of French seriously, answering questions in either
language, saying he intends to invest the $1,000 grant
Katimavik gives participants who complete the program
into a French immersion course in Chicoutimi.

That night, before turning in, Anthony and I watch the day's footage on the camcorder's small screen. Here are some thoughts from Liam Pierce:

"Katimavik helped me change and grow. Now, I'm not as afraid when I have to speak before a group ... In this program, we don't have a choice: we continually have to deal with others, to discuss, shout, agree ... The most important thing I learned? How to accept my surroundings ... Accepting things as they are, adapting to them and changing with them ..."

His thoughts on his country?

"I think being Canadian is wonderful. We're a wonderful people, a beautiful country ... Friendly ... Anyone can come to live here ... For example, in my hometown, Prince George, our 90,000 or so citizens are from various cultures and, on the whole, there's no discrimination ... For me, that's wonderful! I love the people, and believe Canada to be a good country, whose ideal is to welcome all people without discrimination. For this reason, our country could really be a model for the world ... "

And to say that some friends can't understand why we don't need a TV on board ...

Next stop: Rivière-Ouelle. Anthony discovers the rugged beauty of the lower South Shore. A picnic by the sea side— as they call the river around here—redolent with salt air and the strong scent of kelp.

We drive through Saint-Pascal, where I spent four years of my childhood, at my grandmother's, between the ages of 8 and 12. A thousand memories, including that of a first love—unrequited naturally!

Here again, participants are scattered among their host families. We visit one of them, who operates a dairy farm.

Near Rivière-Ouelle, Quebec, Anthony discovers the beauty of the lower South Shore.

Over the last two years, three times a year, Bérangère Goulet and Gilles Martin host a participant for two weeks. The one they're now taking in (the sixth) is a tall Jeff from Ontario. He makes noble efforts to speak French with his hosts and with us.

Dinner with the project leader and Roger Richard, mayor of Rivière-Ouelle. At the moment, he's hosting Hina Zaidi at his home, a Montreal girl of Pakistani extraction. A strong Katimavik supporter, the mayor will bring the municipality's guest book to tonight's special celebration, with host families and their participants, at the Katimavik house: "I need everyone's signature!"

At about 7:00 p.m., there must be thirty or so of us gathered in the kitchen-dining room. The huge table is covered with delicacies prepared by participants... and the mayor's wife! We trade anecdotes, discuss and laugh.

"This really feels like a Christmas party!" says the mayor, alluding to the family atmosphere stirring this house in the old part of Rivière-Ouelle.

I congratulate Hina on her pastries and insist on the quality of the bread, which is often good and always different from one Katimavik house to the next. The project leader, Claude Hudon, provides a fitting anecdote: "The other day, I told Jeff and Patrick it was their turn to bake bread. They strongly protested by admitting— the horror! —they'd never baked any. That night, Jeff and Patrick showed me their bread. Marvellous! One of the best we'd eaten, which leads me to believe this wasn't their first experience."

Hina Zaidi on right with the mayor of Rivière-Ouelle, Roger Richard.

Seated beside me, Jeff has a sly smile and whispers in my ear: "I just have to tell you something ... " Since Patrick and he really didn't know how to bake bread, and had no desire to learn that day, they went to the supermarket to buy some. "With our money!" he specifies. "We placed it in a pan and presented it to the project leader, who was absolutely delighted. The other participants were completely taken in!"

A sunset in Rivière-Ouelle, behind the Katimavik house.

The two of us have a good laugh for a few moments. I then suggest to Jeff he confess his hoax to the audience, so we're not the only ones having fun. Without hesitating too much, Jeff stands, assumes an air of bogus remorse and admits the truth, triggering a volley of widespread laughter.

July 10

I visit Rivière-Ouelle's municipal campground, locus of the work project for a Saskatchewan participant. She gives me a tour of the facility, but suddenly stops to say:

"Sometimes participants complain about the strictness of Katimavik's rules concerning drugs, alcohol and sex. I don't. Before participating in Katimavik, I had a serious drug problem. I know that with the least infraction, without a shadow of a warning, I'll be sent back home. I care too much about the program to take such a risk. I'm now through with drugs."

For his part, Anthony interviews Jeffrey Mintz, the tall Jeff from Phelpston, Ontario.

"I'd read the brochures before leaving, but they don't tell you much … When I arrived in the program, I quickly understood that, to survive, you had to establish good relations with the others. Otherwise, nothing goes right. For example, if you don't respect the people in your group, you'd best be elsewhere. All the same, any disrespect leads to dismissal. At the beginning of the program, I got a final warning from the project leader. Which means that with the next breach of the respect rule I'll be sent home, to Ontario."

Jeff assumes a grave expression:

"That's when I had to answer the question: do I want to experience Katimavik, yes or no? The answer was yes, because I knew I needed this program. In such a vast world, filled with so many different people and distinct cultures, we must adapt and see things as others do... I was disrespectful to my group by merely refusing to perform my share of the tasks. Yet the guys and girls I live with are all terrific, wonderful. I finally understood that the problem with the group was me. And then I changed. Now all the participants say they're really proud of me ... Yes, and I'm proud of myself as well! And proud to be doing this program, which is a lot more intense than I imagined. I didn't know we'd work so much, even on weekends ... At first, I felt a little like an exploited slave! Then I understood that I was learning how to work and, especially, to work with others ... In the group and in the community ... You meet tons of people ... Working and living go hand in hand!"

Jeff admits he's no longer the same:

Jeffrey Mintz from Phelpston, Ontario: "I'm now proud of myself!"

"I wanted to change, really become myself, gain maturity, see Canada, discover another side of the world ... You remain rather ignorant if you grow up in the same small town, without ever leaving it ... with the possible exception of vacationing in Florida with your family! And you'll have gone to school your whole life, without ever going elsewhere, seeing something else ...

Katimavik really broadens your mind. And then you take responsibility for your own life!"

Jeff was a convinced dropout, but everyone constantly tells him to go back to school:

"You won't go anywhere without school! Fine. After Katimavik, I think I'll consider that option... " Jeff concludes, with a dreamy expression.

On the road to Saint-Onésime, in the hinterland. A small village I'd never yet seen. A familiar scenario: a grand celebration with the ten participants and ten host families, gathered in the huge Katimavik house, a former rectory, now abandoned. Mayor Jacques Dionne will join us with his wife, Brigitte Pelletier, who'd been a participant in 1984!

An evening filled with laughter, very much like the one held last night. Once again, we get the strong feeling of belonging to a huge extended family.

A farmer, his face tanned by the sun and the air in the fields, suddenly turns serious and launches into an incredible tirade:

"It's completely crazy to shut kids away inside the four walls of a classroom from kindergarten to university! They have no contact with real life, don't know what's going on elsewhere and, soon as they're 16 or 17 years old, are asked to make choices and decisions that will trap them in one type of career or another till they die. We should categorically replace one year of highschool with one year of Katimavik. For everyone! Make it compulsory! That would darn well change our society!"

I feel like I'm dreaming, since I've repeated pretty much the same speech hundreds of times since the founding of Katimavik, though I'm against any form of compulsory program.

According to research carried out in the United States by the Gallup Institute, and adapted to the Canadian population, we estimate that 50,000 young Canadians would *voluntarily* sign up for Katimavik each year. Such a number would no doubt compel education departments to count that year as a school year.

Our friend from Saint-Onésime is quite right: our society would then change in depth … indeed!

Anthony interviews Gabrielle Laroche, a young girl from Papineauville, Quebec. As he always does, he alternates between French and English questions, to assess the linguistic proficiency of participants.

The following are a few excerpts from Gabrielle's comments:

"I don't really know how to explain it, but the group is a second family to me. I learned a great deal about myself because of it, which helped me change One of the best experiences in my life!"

Anthony switches to English, which doesn't bother Gabrielle in the least:

"My English goes very well, I think I learned a lot in Katimavik. Certainly more than in school! I really love my

Gabrielle Laroche from Papineauville, Quebec: "The group is my second family!"

hometown, Papineauville. Oh! It's really small! Really, really small. But I love my town, I love my family, I love my friends … But I was wanting to go somewhere else, to learn new things, and see new stuff, see other trees, other towns, other people, other cultures … And that's what I did with Katimavik and it's great! I love it! "

A long conversation with Kevin Lutzac from Rivierview, New Brunswick, "the only bilingual province in Canada," he stipulates. Besides, one of the reasons that made him join Katimavik was to perfect his French:

Kevin Lutzac from Riverview, N.B.: "After highschool, I didn't know where to go ..."

"Following highschool, I really didn't know what to do with myself ... I certainly wanted to discover other parts of the country, meet completely different people, learn French and new work skills ... That's what Katimavik is there for ... We have Internet access, but there are no TVs in Katimavik houses. So, instead of wasting our time watching it, as does everyone, we do productive things, we read, write, learn a great deal by talking among ourselves, by organizing group activities in the evening."

July 11

We avoid the oh-so-lovely Highway 20, preferring the 132, which is winding, wild, romantic, and will allow Anthony to discover the most beautiful villages of the lower Saint

Lawrence. We lunch on Alfredo pasta in Montmagny, over-looking the "sea" which is still set off by the dark silhou-ettes of Île aux Grues and Grosse-Île.

We head away from the river, once again plunging into the rolling hinterland in search of a tiny village called Saint-Margloire, where one of our experimental Leader programs (16 to 19 years of age) has taken refuge.

Dinner with the group. More pasta, but Anthony and I must agree the spaghetti prepared by participants is far superi-or to the Alfredo in a packet we had at noon. A young fran-cophone from Ottawa, Olivier Jarvis, monopolizes our attention:

"We've been together barely two weeks," he says, "but feel like we've always known each other. I'm sure we'll be friends for life." The others agree without hesitation ...

There is a Katimavik work site in the area...

As we're having coffee, the mayor of Saint-Margloire and three municipal councillors join us. They adore Katimavik, but would like to host a regular seven-month program (or longer) rather than one lasting only six weeks.

July 12

Breakfast with participants. Olivier says that, as soon as he returns to Ottawa, he'll commit himself to promoting Katimavik, write letters to MPs, get signatures on petitions, etc. He wants to become a politician. Great! The day when a majority of MPs are former participants, we'll have fewer budget problems!

Meanwhile, we must pick up our pilgrim's staff, continue approaching as many Canadians as possible and, if need be, convince them one at a time about the virtues of Katimavik!

First real day of summer. A hot wind, the voluptuous hills of the Saint Lawrence basin rolling against a deep-blue sky.

We reach Montreal before noon. I drop Anthony off at his home—though he professes to be a New Brunswicker, he's been an adopted Montrealer for the last eight years. He has some business to settle, particularly with respect to the video, and fully deserves a few days rest.

Since our departure, we've awakened between 6:00 and 7:00 a.m., with Anthony often grinding away on the computer till midnight. Day after day, he's at the wheel. I replaced him a few times when he asked me to, especially since I wanted to avoid giving him the opportunity of boasting some day that he drove for the *whole* trip!

Let's admit Anthony is a good driver, able to travel 700 kilometres and more without showing fatigue. He seems to love this and, no doubt, feels less secure when I replace him at the wheel … How right he is!

I'm delighted to see Alain again, the trip coordinator, who'll relieve Anthony over the next few days.

At 4:00 p.m. we hit the road to briefly visit (too briefly!) an experimental LeaderPlus group (for participants between 22 and 26), located in East Hereford in the Townships. Participants are hard at work preparing a huge fruit salad for tomorrow's picnic with other participants in the area at Coaticook's parc des Gorges. So long! See you tomorrow!

July 13

Katimavik is intimately linked to the history of this park, one of the region's most beautiful. That's why we aren't surprised that the celebrations include the area's three mayors (Coaticook, East Hereford and Saint-Herménégilde). Three enthusiasts who are well aware that, without Katimavik, this park might not exist.

Our guests include a man who knows a great deal about the subject: Claude Raîche, an old pioneer and member of Katimavik's board. He reminds the three mayors that Katimavik's very first group came here in 1977, when the Coaticook Gorges were still undeveloped. When the mayor at the time had claimed he could find no useful work for participants, Claude Raîche, then regional director for Quebec, told him: "Why don't you develop the Coaticook Gorges and turn them into a tourist attraction? They're at least as spectacular as Ausable Chasm! …"

At the Coaticook Gorges, with the three local mayors and Claude Raîche (in the background). Photo Alain Choinière.

Still somewhat sceptical, the mayor had allowed participants to build a first footpath giving hikers access to the gorges. Over the years, other participants contributed to laying out one of the most spectacular parks in the Townships.

Twenty-three years after the first Katimavik group, another continues to beautify the grounds, where some forty guests will treat themselves to the fruit salad from East Hereford and to the rest of the picnic.

As for me, I have neither time to eat nor chat with our guests: I give interviews nonstop for over an hour: television, radio, dailies, weeklies ... They'll hear about the School of Life around here!

On the way back, we drop in on Senator Léonce Mercier, who has continually supported Katimavik with unfailing determination. We talk about politics and the possibility of general elections, laughing heartily for a good while, since the senator is the funniest of storytellers.

July 17

Still with Alain, we quickly drop in on a group located in another enchanting park, near Sainte-Scholastique. Just long enough to share a curried lentil stew and a few conclusive words on the future of the world.

Settling the world's fate in Sainte-Scholastique, Quebec … Photo Alain Choinière.

July 18

I reunite with Anthony in Montreal, finding him rested and refreshed. We have barely two months of travelling left ...

Next stop: Sainte-Marthe, a tiny village hosting a group working in the area.

As agreed, we reach the Katimavik house at 7:00 p.m. It's completely deserted: another huge old rectory, at one

time bustling with activity (three garages!), but which hasn't seen a priest in donkey's years.

A welcome note pinned to the door informs us the group may be a few minutes late, held back outside Sainte-Marthe due to a "workshop about the job market." A serious reason, naturally!

We later find out we were expected at 9:00 p.m., not 7:00 p.m. ... Participants arrive ten minutes early, at 8:50 p.m. ...

In one of the rectory's huge sitting rooms, we trade stories while savouring a fantastic frozen dessert prepared by Bhushan Crosman, a tall skinny fellow from Victoria, on kitchen duty this week. He also wants to get into politics some day: he thinks I'm just the man to give him useful advice ... Oh, the touching candour of youth!

Breakfast with Sainte-Marthe participants.

July 19

At 7:30 a.m., a very special breakfast in our honour prepared by Bhushan and Lisa: pancakes and maple syrup (genuine), stewed rhubarb (picked in the rectory's gardens). I treat myself to a slice of whole-wheat bread which Bhushan kneaded yesterday: if politics doesn't suit him, he's got a great future in the bakery business!

Chapter 5

BETHUNE'S WAY

Ontario

July 19

Eight-thirty a.m. Before us stretches the long road to Hamilton, where we'll arrive a little before 6:00 p.m. Three groups to meet. Someone had the good idea of gathering them around a large wood fire. A kind of picnic that inevitably ends with marshmallows skewered at the tip of

Lunch time, on the road to Hamilton, Ontario.

thin twigs ... and which are allowed to burn to a cinder amid the flames. Participants then swallow the darkened puffs ... while evoking the cancer awaiting consumers of carbon!

Between marshmallows, Paul Griffith from Newfoundland suddenly blurts out: "Katimavik is the best thing that ever happened in my life!"

Daniel Shipp, the coordinator, drags us along on a whirl-wind tour: he wants to show us all the work projects participants are engaged in, particularly the Dundas Valley Conservation Area, a lovely stretch of forest known as "Carolinian" since it features vegetation typical of the Carolinas, which are much farther south.

A long stroll with John Bryden, a former colleague in Parliament and MP for the region. He's a good friend of Katimavik and feels completely at ease with participants, inviting them for a hike through this historic place whose every secret he knows.

A huge picnic at the Merrick Field Centre, near Hamilton.

On the way to the patch of forest where the Hamilton group is working.

A meeting with a group whose task is to help YMCA counsellors with children between the ages of 6 and 10 who've come to spend a day in the park.

Cameron, one of our handicapped participants, manages along in his wheelchair: the children love him!

A narrow dirt road leads us into a thick forest, where other participants are helping with a more spectacular project, the Children's Rehabilitation Development Program of Hamilton. It works by helping children confined to wheelchairs climb very high into trees using cables and pulleys.

By playing Tarzan, these young people learn to control their fears and acquire greater self confidence.

In the evening, a campfire with Friends of Katimavik from the area. Babies, grandmothers and dogs have been brought along. The more cautious parties brought folding chairs since participants informed us they were organizing a show, of the type that always lasts longer than expected.

Participants help handicapped youth overcome their fears.

Divided into five groups corresponding to the five regions of the country, participants extravagantly praise their region with songs, skits and improvisations ... before an audience that's already won over!

Each team has the mission of convincing the four others that their region is the best in the country. Dumbfounded young Ontarians learn with great dismay that "Montmorency Falls, near Quebec City, are higher than Niagara Falls" (something I hadn't previously known!) and that "Quebec has given Céline Dion and poutine to the world" (I already knew ...).

July 21

Following a four-hour drive, we reach the Gravenhurst Katimavik house. It's empty, as we'd been informed: participants are with their host families, dispersed throughout the village.

A picnic has been organized in the yard which, soon, will be filled with participants, host families, partners and other friends, with the mayor leading the way. He informs me—as have all mayors met so far—that his municipal council will pass a resolution praising Katimavik and recommending its rapid expansion. He'll send copies to the Department of Heritage and to the Federation of Canadian Municipalities.

Among the partners attending, a representative from the house—now a historic site—where Doctor Norman Bethune was born. A long-unsung Canadian hero, he

They abandon their wheelchairs to play Tarzan in Creiff Hills, Ontario.

With the local press in Gravenhurst, Ontario.

remains controversial to this day. This modest house has become a major tourist attraction, especially among the Chinese: they worship this Canadian physician who wore himself out and died taking care of Mao Tse-tung's soldiers during the Long March.

In 1960, during a trip to China with a few friends, I discovered that Bethune was a major hero to nearly a billion Chinese. To the schedule suggested by our tiny group, our hosts had felt it was essential to add a detour whose only purpose was to show us where the great Bethune died and is buried.

Alison Frie, a participant from Medicine Hat, Alberta, in fact works at the Bethune House and at its adjoining museum: she's only too glad to accompany us there.

The period decor has been reconstituted very authentically. And realistically to the point of putting fresh lettuce in the salad bowl!

Inside the museum, the great moments of Bethune's life are described, as well as the lesser-known aspects of his prodigious work. Everyone knows he took part in the Spanish Civil War on the Republican side, and in the Long March as part of Mao's inner circle. What isn't as well-known are his talents as an inventor, which gave us surgical instruments so well designed they're still being used.

An outstanding humanist, tireless surgeon, poet, painter and passionate defender of health insurance—way before it was popular! On the walls are some of his pithy phrases:

Geneviève Buron from Trois-Rivières, Quebec, a participant in the Gravenhurst group.

"There is no such thing as private health—all health is public."

"There is a rich man's tuberculosis and a poor man's tuberculosis. The rich man recovers and the poor man dies."

A night in Gravenhurst next to the Katimavik house, which is obviously uninhabited. We take the liberty of connecting our electric cable to it, as well as our water hose.

July 22

In Parry Sound and Huntsville, Katimavik houses are deserted as well. We'll therefore get to meet host families, their participants and friends during a picnic or reception.

Anthony, camcorder forever in hand, interviews several participants, including Caroline Dufour from Val d'Or, Quebec. She talks about group living and its hardships.

In her opinion, the key is to understand people around you, to listen to others, to have a positive attitude ... "To accept that people around you are different, and always be ready to change your ideas to be able to communicate ..."

Caroline has really discovered Canada: "I don't think I really knew my country ... I'm from Quebec ... I only spoke French ... But when you cross the language barrier, you realize we're all alike ... We all resemble one another. It's important for us to open up to others, to learn from others, from English Canadians, for example ... Canada is a wonderful country!"

Does Caroline want to change things with the world? She feels people should adopt a new attitude towards the envi-

Caroline Dufour from Val d'Or, Quebec, in Parry Sound, Ontario.

ronment, that they should think with their heart and forget money: "We have to know how to give with our hearts, open up to others and bring them something new …"

Quite a program, dear Caroline!

July 23

Same story in South River and North Bay: we're still in the period when participants spend two weeks with their host families.

Receptions, friends, mayors, notables, local press. We don't get bored, even if events are similar from day to day. One thing's never the same: participants, their reactions, discoveries and emotions. The following excerpts from an interview with Jonathan Duclos from Val-Bélair, Quebec, testify to this:

Jonathan Duclos from Val-Bélair, Quebec: "I learned to respect absolutely everything!"

"I came into contact with different Canadian cultures. For example, in Prince Edward Island, I worked with francophone Acadians... Then in Okotoks, Alberta, with cowboys..."

To Jonathan, the world's most serious problem is war, often caused by religious intolerance: "What's missing is respect for others ... Well, this is something we learn in Katimavik: you respect the group leader, participants, the house, your room, nature ... You learn to respect absolutely everything!"

Before Katimavik, as is the case for many young people his age, Jonathan didn't know what he wanted to do later in life. Through some mysterious development he's just discovered his vocation: he'll be a luthier: "Oh, the repairing of violins and guitars ..."

To gain some time, we'll camp in Sturgeon Falls, next to the Katimavik house, which is empty as well. We'll be at ease using the washer, dryer, showers and the computer which allows Anthony to send news about us to the four corners of the country, in the form of photos with comments.

July 24

With the city mayor, we visit the location of a Katimavik work project: the Sturgeon River House Park and Museum. The mayor, Garry O'Connor, informs me he'll make an appeal in support of Katimavik before a meeting of 300 delegates from Franco-Ontarian communities, to be held in two days at Rivière-des-Français. Meanwhile, he gives a remarkable speech before the assembled participants and notables. Slowly, but surely, we're gaining ground…

Anthony interviews a wonderful participant, Kelly Julseth, from Terrace, British Columbia. We listen to her and watch her on the screen of the video camera, our tiny 2" by 3" TV… Kelly has a smile that could charm a grizzly bear. No doubt the reason she was put in charge of organizing the three meetings in South River, North Bay and Sturgeon Falls.

Visiting the work site with the mayor of Sturgeon Falls, Ontario.

Kelly has much to say, but what's striking is her sense of wonder towards Canada, the diversity of the nature and culture in each province: "Thanks to Katimavik, I've

Kelly Julseth from Terrace, B.C.: "You have to have an open mind ..."

become much more patriotic than I'd ever been ... before leaving British Columbia!"

It's late, we're sleepy, but can't resist the temptation of watching two more interviews.

Tom Skerritt, from Mississauga, Ontario, looks at the bright side of things. He's the embodiment of the perfect partici-pant. Proud of his group, as he should be: "A very quiet group, better organised than the others ... We managed to establish strong friendships. Nothing superficial!"

For Tom, Katimavik is more than a program: it's the School of Life: "Discoveries, trips, all the cool people you meet ...

We laugh with the North Bay group.

Posing for the North Bay Nugget reporter.

Tom Skerritt from Mississauga, Ontario: "We managed to establish strong friendships ..."

The Katimavik house in North Bay, Ontario.

Katimavik is a lifestyle! All you learn living as a group of eleven people in a house for seven months is incalculable. And it'll stay with us to the end of our days..."

Alison Bergman from Guelph, Ontario: "I really needed to get out of Guelph!"

We close the evening—and this long day!—with Alison Bergman from Guelph, Ontario.

She first tells us about what she learned working as a volunteer. At a woodworking shop in Saint-Onésime, a tiny village near Quebec City, at a Métis historic site at Lac La Biche in northern Alberta and, finally, at the Sturgeon Falls Museum ... "I learned a great deal!"

Does Katimavik meet her expectations?

"Way more than I could've imagined. It's also more structured, with rules for behaviour and everything, group living, daily chores around the house ... I loved it!"

"I've spent my whole life in Guelph, Ontario. I was sick and tired of always being in the same house, seeing the same friends. I really needed to get out of it, to experience new things. That's the main reason I signed up with Katimavik...

The view in front of the Montreal River Harbour Campsite.

I finally learned to judge things for myself, without being influenced by my parents or my Guelph friends ... I learned and grew, especially in the moral sense ..."

We end up in a rather ordinary campground near Montreal River. As a general rule, we try to choose the most spectacular campsites, such as those found in national and provincial parks. Even if we have to drive several kilometres more ...

Similarly, at lunch time, we'll strive to find a lovely river, a tiny unexpected lake, or the magical expanse of a ripened wheat field. Frugal meals, but with a view: a somewhat lordly predilection!

Tonight, we forget the shortcomings of the campground's sanitary arrangements by admiring the dazzling phantasmagoria of a sunset over Lake Superior ...

July 25

Phone call from Alain. He gives us the schedule of our meetings in Alberta ... which seems at the end of the earth to us!

Unfortunately, the 1999-2000 program is drawing to a close and, to avoid missing any of the groups still in the field, somewhere in Canada, we'll have to gain time: instead of spending the night in the Thunder Bay area as planned, we speed along westbound till we reach Torque Provincial Park, near the small town of Ignacio.

An 843 kilometre day! Anthony refuses to hand me the wheel and only stops when his videographer's instinct prompts him to shoot a scene, a beautiful house, even a bee.

A frugal meal with a view!

A violent thunderstorm. We have to stop a while. Lightning, thunder, blinding rain. Likely to remind us we're near Thunder Bay!

We reach Lake Superior Provincial Park at 8:00 p.m.! A mistake! It's really only 7:00 p.m., since we just moved into a new time zone. What an incredible country! To cover it from end to end, we'll have to cross six time zones!

Sunset over Lake Superior.

July 26

A beautiful region of sweeping hills dotted with a thousand lakes stretches between Thunder Bay and the Manitoba border. Feels like being in the Laurentians.

In the vicinity of Thunder Bay, Ontario.

Soon as we reach Manitoba, the landscape changes, as though a huge iron had just flattened the hills. Only fields, far as the eye can see on either side of a rectilinear road dreamed up by surveyors.

Still, before we reach Brandon, a few timid hillocks with a fleeting appearance: they'll disappear before day's end.

We camp at the city gates in a pleasant underwood.

A bee gathering nectar and pollen by the roadside, Thunder Bay, Ontario.

Chapter 6

THE WIDE,
EVER-CHANGING PLAIN

Manitoba, Saskatchewan, Alberta

July 27

Another good day: 560 kilometres over a road having few curves, between Brandon and Moose Jaw.

The Assiniboine River, on the road to Brandon, Manitoba.

Contrary to a persistent legend, the great plain that stretches to the Rockies isn't dreary. No more so, in any event, than the middle of the ocean or the Sahara. Because they're unusual, any uneven patches of ground, fences, trees or porcupines become a display.

Kilometres of level fields, a gleaming quilt where yellow, green and ochre prevail, all of which places you in a better perspective. Likely the reason deserts, endless plains and oceans attract individuals seeking the infinite.

Whatever anyone says, there's always something to see. Like the humble wildflowers that ceaselessly amaze us with their diversity. At times modest, discreet and pastel-hued, at times flamboyant, and restless as friars' lanterns.

We occasionally stop by the roadside just to look at them closely, and photograph them lovingly, to pick a few, with every consideration due to the environment. Since we left, the table where we eat and work has always known the joy of a small bouquet of wildflowers, whose light fragrance prolongs the recollection of passing days.

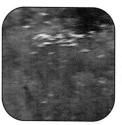

Time to pick a few wildflowers...

We reach the Moose Jaw Katimavik house around 6:00 p.m., after crossing all of Manitoba and half of Saskatchewan nearly nonstop! ... A crime if we hadn't planned to take our time on the way back ... in a month and a half!

A wonderful group of cheerful participants was expecting us for the dinner prepared by Jay Nathan from Toronto, and Ryan MacWha from Berwick, Nova Scotia. Two guys

A freshly picked bouquet to brighten up breakfast!

not afraid of cooking for the fourteen people expected tonight. Moreover, they'll have to bake seven dozen muffins and rolls for tomorrow's outdoor breakfast, a welcoming ceremony presided over by the mayor of Moose Jaw.

Jay is eighteen-years old and interested in everything, including Canadian politics and the fate of the world. He speaks with a passion rather unusual for people his age. Naturally, he's heading straight for political science and journalism and, who knows, perhaps active politics. Should he run some day, he can count on me for the door-to-door canvassing ...

July 28

At 10:00 a.m., a meeting beneath a vast pavilion in the middle of a municipal park. The usual scenario, with a speech from Mayor Ray Boughen, interviews with the local press, etc.

To entertain guests, some participants have devised a game called *Katimavik Pursuit*. Questions test the knowledge of players concerning Katimavik, Saskatchewan and Moose Jaw in particular.

The quiz master is Ryan, who comes from the depths of Nova Scotia. He's got an amazing work project: he gives out information about Moose Jaw and its surroundings at the tourist centre:

Ryan MacWha from Berwick, N.S., met in Moose Jaw, Saskatchewan.

"So how much information can you give? You just barely got to this city!"

"I learned quickly!" he answers, laughing.

The brunch welcoming us with the mayor of Moose Jaw.

The mayor will get his council to vote a resolution supporting Katimavik!

With the happy Moose Jaw group.

In Saskatoon, with Howard Nixon, first co-president of Katimavik in 1977.

On the road, heading northwest, through checkerboard fields … flat as the whole world was before Galileo! A few heavy tractors hop in the distance, barely visible, and look like hardworking bumblebees.

Next appointment: the regional office for the Prairie Provinces in Saskatoon. A convivial meeting with staff, well managed by Catherine Laratte. A press conference, crustless sandwiches and pastries.

Near Moose Jaw, an ocean of tiny blue flowers.

A visit of work projects in Saskatoon: a children's camp and a house renovated for needy families.

In the evening, we attend a celebration in the yard behind the house of one of the city's two groups. I'm extremely pleased to see Howard Nixon again. He's a great humanitarian and well-known Saskatoon personality who co-presided Katimavik with me at the very beginning.

I also renew acquaintance with two participants from 1978: Janet Clark and her sister Mary. Laughing, they recall the good times and difficulties of those first experiences. At the time, a group consisted of 33 participants ... living in the same house! You can imagine the huge problems that

At the celebration in Saskatoon, Janet and Nancy Clark, participants in 1978...

presupposes, but the Clark sisters have kept only fond memories. (By the next year, we'd understood that groups of eleven would be more manageable!)

"Thanks to Katimavik," says Janet, "I was able to discover many regions of the country, and make friends in every corner of Canada ... "

She speaks with emotion of a Christmas day once spent in Quebec City:

"I had friends who were Quebecers, and that was very important to me ... Following Katimavik, I was able to work in various regions of the country because I felt at home everywhere ... My generation no longer define themselves exclusively by the region of Canada they live in or by the province where they were born, or even by their social class ... We create bonds with people around the world, we adopt a more universal attitude ... And that's how I see the future!"

We'd agreed to turn in early, given tomorrow's long journey. But dragging ourselves away from these terrific boys and girls before 11:00 p.m. is difficult ...

July 29

Up at 6:00 a.m. To save time, we said farewell to participants last night, all of whom are surely asleep inside their large quiet house next to which we'd parked ours.

We head towards Edmonton, Calgary and especially Okotoks, where a group is located.

A brief stop by the Saskatchewan River: a quick wash, juice, cereal, yogourt. But the view! The view!

We reach Alberta at about 10:00 p.m., barely grazing Edmonton and Calgary, where we'll stop on our return. For the moment, we head straight for Okotoks, with a few

The prairie, forever the prairie, in Alberta.

wrong turnoffs, as though Calgary won't let us turn our backs on it!

In the distance, at the end of fields carpeted with yellow flowers, stands the steel-blue silhouette of the Rockies. Treasures that cause terrible pangs of envy among Canadians who can't see them from their porches!

In Okotoks, we'd discover an exceptional group of 11 par-

At the house in Okotoks, Alberta, Heather Moss serves coffee.

ticipants, which hasn't yet lost any of its members for breaking the rules or other causes. They're proud as peacocks, teaming with energy and the joy of still being together after nearly seven months.

We have a great time with them, and Anthony would like to do video interviews with each one of these strong and interesting characters.

Located right in the middle of a residential neighbourhood,

Karine Taillon from Longueuil, Quebec, learned English: "My best friend is from Vancouver!"

the Katimavik house doesn't have a space for us to park our vehicle for the night. So we'll camp on the street, right in front. As for water and electricity, we're okay: our reserves allow us complete autonomy for a day or two. But discretion is in order to avoid having the police tell us to clear off. We watch the day's interviews in any event.

Karine Taillon is from Quebec. A beaming participant if ever there was one! A little sad, however, at the thought this wonderful dream is drawing to a close and that she'll have to part with her group:

"We've grown into a big family. All brothers and sisters now… There's no awkwardness left among us… It's really fantastic… A second family that will be with you the rest of your life!"

Karine continues in her brand new English, something that would have been impossible before Katimavik:

"Never before did I have friends who couldn't speak my language. It's weird! Just like … Hey! Wow! … I can communicate with someone who doesn't speak French … And we can be friends … Actually, my best friend in the group is an anglophone from Vancouver. So, it's like amazing!"

Frédéric Bossé is very proud of his roots:

"I'm from the Saguenay, right from Jonquière, in Quebec!"

Like Karine, he learned English with the group, discovered new provinces, wonderful places, terrific people … But especially, he discovered what he wants to do with his life… without really telling us!

Frédéric Bossé from Jonquière, Quebec, discovered what he wanted to do with his life...

Kim Mills from Moosomin, Saskatchewan, is more loquacious:

"When I was at school, I wanted to become a psychologist… "

Kim Mills from Moosomin, Saskatchewan, in Okotoks: "I discovered here that I liked to work with children …"

But following very stimulating work experiences over the last few months, she changed her mind:

"I discovered I liked working with children and the handi-capped … What I've just experienced has opened my mind and made me discover my own potential … "

July 30

Eight a.m. A wonderful breakfast with, as usual, a group of friends, municipal councillors, local journalists, and the families who hosted a participant for two weeks, a fasci-nating experience for both families and participants.

The tragedy of this trip is that we only get to know these young people superficially. Barely do we have time to learn their first names, to find out that Heather has suffered a sprain, that a wisdom tooth is causing poor Josh some pain... Then we're off!

Dinner with the Red Deer group, a little less cheerful than the one from Okotoks, and why we'll never know. Perhaps the group has some problem, but participants aren't doing too badly, judging from their testimonies.

The words of Emily Cook, an Ottawa participant, lead us to believe that the group's life hasn't always been easy:

"A constant challenge... Endless arguments... Ordeals to

Emily Cook from Ottawa: "Katimavik opened my eyes to science and the environment."

go through ... Simply living together, 24 hours a day, for six or seven months! ... Definitely like building a new family... But, in our own family, we feel accepted, at ease... What's

Benoît Baribeau from Chateauguay, Quebec, a participant with the Red Deer group.

certain is that you can't pretend to be someone you're not!"

Before Katimavik, Emily had absolutely no interest in science. In one of her work projects, at the BC Museum of the Environment, she discovered practical applications for using science to protect the environment:

"It opened my eyes to the importance of science and to the urgency of protecting our natural resources."

Benoît Baribeau is from Chateauguay and from Quebec especially, a province for which he feels strong passion:

"Nothing is more beautiful than Quebec! But it's worthwhile going to other provinces to see what we don't have in ours. I really liked the mountains in British Columbia... Not so much the mosquitoes in Alberta ... I saw some of the Prairies ... "

In personal terms, Benoît is rather pleased with what's happening to him:

"Oh, I feel I've grown a lot... I acquired greater maturity. Now I can solve problems without telling someone off. I'm really able to speak!"

At first, Benoît was extremely self-absorbed:

"I'd only speak to the Quebecers in the group. I slowly opened up to the anglophones... Katimavik taught me how to communicate with others, to respect everyone... "

Guylaine Harvey is a participant from Longueuil, Quebec. Her words suggest that group living has had its ups and downs. But she has excellent memories of the Rockies, is proud to have learned English (and patience!) and to have had a thousand rewarding experiences.

Since only two weeks are left in the program, Guylaine is

Guylaine Harvey from Longueuil, Quebec: "I'm afraid I'll feel very lonely when I get back home ..."

starting to look forward to seeing her family and friends in Longueuil again:

"I'm looking forward to it, but, at the same time, I don't know how I'll react when I'm alone at home ... Far from the people with whom I've lived for seven months and have gotten used to ... I think I'll feel very lonely ... far from Jonathan who plays guitar, from Stéphanie, with whom I speak all the time, from Benoît, with whom I argue ... It'll be strange ... "

July 31

At 10:00 a.m., we get a most exuberant welcome from the Camrose group, a small town in the heart of Alberta. The Katimavik house is teaming with participants and friends, including Leroy Johnson, a member of the provincial assembly: his family hosted participants very recently.

We talk to everyone, and a little more with Marc-André Boucher, a tall fellow from Sorel, Quebec, who's somewhat of a poet. This is how he describes Katimavik:

"It was like a flower ... At the beginning of the program, we were like the roots of a plant about to sprout from the ground ... In North Bay, during the first rotation, we began to water the plant, which then started to grow, to thrive, producing a beautiful blossom in the end ... A very rewarding experience when each adds a little of their own water!"

Marc-André is rather proud of his recent experience, which included learning to speak English:

"Before I left Sorel, my country was Quebec... Canada was like something else... There was Quebec and the rest of

Canada... Now that I've seen Canada, I know it's a united country. I was a little more separatist when I started... I've seen we're not so different... We're all the same and can get along so well... In French, in English, whatever, it's the same ... There are differences, but we're all pretty much the same... For example, there are no Quebecers, or

Marc-André Boucher from Sorel, Quebec, has come to plant flowers in Camrose...

Manitobans or Newfoundlanders in our group... We're just a Katimavik team, right now... "

We take leave of the group at noon, and head for another one, in Bonnyville, a small town a few kilometres farther north.

To avoid changing anything in their schedule, we join participants in the activity planned for the evening: a drill at

Bonnyville's volunteer fire station. Very seriously, as though there were a fire, the firemen help us don fire-proof costumes and place enormous oxygen tanks on our backs. We have trouble walking… And I'm beginning to feel a deep sympathy for firemen… which was perhaps the purpose of the exercise!

The highlight: a ride in one of those huge trucks, red as can be, siren raging. We're taken to a rather deserted road so that everyone gets a chance to drive the juggernaut… without running over too many people! Oh, the joy of finally getting to play fireman, every child's dream!

The fire chief gives everyone a T-shirt bearing the crest of the Bonnyville brigade. I'm a little upset: Anthony's T-shirt has the word CHIEF in large white letters. At 77 years of

The group in Camrose, Alberta, with the provincial member, Leroy Johnson.

Playing firefighter with the Bonnyville group in Alberta!

age, I have to settle for being a mere FIREFIGHTER ... There's no justice!

A quiet evening around a fire with participants. Together, often amid a deliberate and refreshing silence, we admire the exploding purpling sunset, a splendid display of the Prairie Provinces, "where there's nothing to see!"

Marshmallows quiver over flames, laughter rings out from every corner, accompanying the most unexpected confidences, anecdotes, questions. With touching tenderness, two Quebec girls talk about this remote Bonnyville, somewhere in northern Alberta, whose existence, without Katimavik, we'd have never even imagined.

The Bonnyville sunset ranks among the magical memories of my life: it may some day come sweeping back to tear me away from the horror of some dull meeting or the torments of a crowded subway …

August 1

At noon, lunch in the open air at an experimental vegetable garden where some participants are working. Perhaps growing flowers like Marc-André … Forty or so guests. The usual blend of politicians, journalists, host families, etc.

We're guests of the community, which is footing the bill for the splendid buffet that includes a huge cake iced in the colours of Katimavik.

Five or six speeches extolling the program which Bonnyville absolutely wants to host again next year,

In Bonnyville, Alberta, at the experimental greenhouse, where participants have worked.

though we've been in this community for the last three years.

Project leaders give us a complete tour of the greenhouse and gardens, highlighting the achievements of participants.

Talking with Brendan Harrison, a Calgary participant, we realize he fully agrees with me about the program's duration:

Brendan Harrison from Calgary: "A seven-month program is too short!"

"Seven months isn't long enough!" he exclaimed outright. He's convinced that programs lasting only a few weeks—or even a month or two—can't offer worthwhile cultural exchanges:

"You need a lot of time for group members to get comfortable with each other ... To discuss any subject with an open mind ... The question of Quebec separatism, for example ... Time is needed for individuals to develop good relations ... Only then can you really begin to exchange ideas ... "

Does Brendan know that the program lasted nine months when it was created, and that it was unwisely reduced to seven months last year for foolish budgetary reasons?

For their part, our local partners bitterly decry this measure, which leaves participants very little time to accomplish worthwhile things in communities. In short, Katimavik must at all costs return to being a nine-month program. Another battle on the horizon!

A hurried departure for Cold Lake, where the same kind of reception, one every bit as pleasant, awaits us. Lengthy speeches and petits-fours before the glacial silence of this huge lake, bereft of the least ripple.

Dinner at the Katimavik house. Strawberry shortcake.

Carl Desbiens is happy to speak French with me, a fellow Montrealer. But he learned English, the only words of which he knew before Katimavik were "yes" and "no."

"I also learned tons of things: cooking, knitting, composting and a lot about the environment ... At first, I was a little sceptical, thinking the English didn't always like Quebecers. In fact, people like us everywhere. And moreover, a francophone always finds other francophones throughout the country, not just Quebec ... I didn't know that. I even celebrated Saint-Jean-Baptiste in Alberta, in a little village still pretty much francophone. In fact, we were celebrating the French language and not the province of Quebec … "

Carl Desbiens from Montreal: "Wow! I celebrated Saint-Jean-Baptiste in a francophone village in Alberta!"

August 2

Lac La Biche. We meet participants and local personalities at the Lac La Biche Mission, an historic site and workplace for the group.

Our partners, French Canadian or Métis, appear keen on history and resolve to tell us everything about this mission founded in 1853 by Father René Remas, and for a long time run by Father Lacombe, a hero little-known outside the Prairies.

An official visit of all buildings (chapel, schools, sheds,

cabins) repaired with the help of participants who've been working on them for three years.

Éric Seney, a fellow from Quebec, grabs my sleeve:

"You see that window in the school's gable? Well, I'm the one who put it in … !"

He also knows that the school was founded in 1898 by Grey Nuns from Montreal. Éric shows me a flour mill that dates back to 1863.

Now a magnificent park, the Lac La Biche Mission was once a junction of the greatest importance for trappers and other coureurs de bois.

Following a mirthful dinner and lengthy conversations, I retire to our van, parked near the Katimavik house. I'm in

Éric and Simon join us for a chat in the van.

Simon Duval from Saint-Roch-de-l'Achigan, Quebec: "My country is Canada from end to end!"

Michelle Bissonnette from Waterloo, Ontario: "The greatest experience in my life!"

the process of carefully studying the long Lac La Biche-Yellowknife leg of the trip on the map, when someone knocks at the door: Éric and Simon, two Quebec participants, want to chat a little more. They examine the map with me:

"Our country is so vast!" Simon exclaims. He insists:

"And it is indeed *my* country! For years, school teachers had told me that only Quebec is my country. The English? So different from us it's useless trying to get along with them. Now, with what I've just experienced, I know it's not true."

Meanwhile, Anthony has interviewed Michelle Bissonnette, an anglophone from Waterloo, Ontario:

"The greatest experience in my life! It's incredible!"

The rest of the interview is in the same vein and very similar to those of other participants met along the way. Her final words, at least, should be heard by parents, educators, governments:

"I think it's a shame that programs like this one aren't better known and more accessible to young people!"

And what does society expect from people like her?

"Finishing highschool, going to university, getting a degree, settling in the suburbs, having 2.5 children, a dog, a fence ... and a Volvo! If only people knew what kind of experience you can live with Katimavik, absolutely all young people would want to participate!"

Chapter 7

AS GOOD AS AN ADVENTURE ...

The Northwest Territories and the Yukon

August 3

Six a.m. With infinite discretion, to awaken no one, we unplug the hose and electrical wire, our final links to this house in Lac La Biche, filled with wonderful sleeping participants.

In northern Alberta, on the road to Yellowknife.

On the road to Yellowknife! For the first time we feel we're heading off the beaten path and into the *unknown* reaches of the Far North.

Starting at Peace River, even tiny villages grow scarce. As we're about to run out of gas, we stop for directions in a gloomy little store right out of the very Old West. The woman running the establishment, no doubt aboriginal, says we won't find gas before Manning, 45 kilometres away.

"But the fuel gauge has been on empty for quite a while! We'll never be able to drive an extra 45 kilometres!"

Lunch in the forest at Peace River, Alberta.

"You'll make it! You'll make it!" the woman repeats tirelessly, by virtue of what gift of clairvoyance we wonder … Having no choice, we bravely hit the road. But the woman runs after us, waving at us to stop, no doubt stricken with remorse. Totally breathless, she says:

"Do you have a Katimavik registration form?"

"A crateful!"

"It's for my daughter, who'd really like to go this fall."

"She'd better hurry: the deadline's in four days!"

We set off again, still worried about running out of fuel.

A phone call changes our focus: Senator Sharon Carstairs asks for news of our journey. A great friend of Katimavik, she's very interested in this trip. We agree to tell her all about it when we drive back through Winnipeg, in a month.

We're now only ten or so kilometres from Manning. Unbeknownst to me, Anthony discretely removes his foot from the accelerator.

"That's it!" he says gravely ... "We've run out!"

Coasting along, slowly, he parks the vehicle by the road-side. I cheer him up:

"Oh well! Doesn't matter. We can easily walk to Manning and return with a gas can ..."

On the camp-ground at the 60th parallel, a few footprints. Bear or duck?

After a few long minutes, Anthony bursts out laughing and fully presses the accelerator!

Rascal! He had me going ...

The wild immensity of the Northwest Territories.

The trees shrink and shrivel as we head farther north. Up to Manning, thin white birches still form an honour guard on each side of the road. Farther on, scrawny and shivery spruces take over.

At dusk, the border of the Northwest Territories, then a lovely campground, of the rather wild type.

By the river, in the soft earth, tracks no doubt left by bears.

August 4

We follow the edge of Wood Buffalo National Park for 80 kilometres. It's the second largest park in the world and surely the only one having 2,500 bison roaming free. All that's left of the 60 million beasts which, before the white man, were scattered throughout the wide prairies. Natives killed some on occasion, to eat and clothe themselves.

Later, whites and even the Métis slaughtered the enormous herd to sell bison hides, and at times only their tongues, considered a delicacy.

At the end of the 19th century, the 60 million bison had been practically exterminated or driven into the United States. That's when, very late, unfortunately, the Canadian government banned hunting bison, finally creating in 1922 the national park we're now admiring.

Anthony drives with one hand, holding the camcorder in the other: he doesn't want to miss a single little bison showing the tip of its nose. Posters warn us about these

Bisons, along the road to Yellowknife.

powerful mammals, generally harmless, except when they charge a pedestrian or even a vehicle.

The area is desolate so, from now on, we'll fill up every time we see the least shadow of a pump. Next one's in Enterprise, a village of fewer than a hundred residents.

At the gas station's cash desk, a woman customer recognizes me, surely because of my T-Shirt bearing a picture of the Lac La Biche Mission:

The unbelievable Yellowknife sunsets!

"I was the librarian at Lac La Biche and, over the years, have had the pleasure of working with your participants. Many still write to me, including a girl whose name is easy to remember: Alberta …"

"That's really strange! We met her barely a month ago in Quebec, in the small village of Saint-Onésime where her group was located …"

The world of Katimavik is small indeed!

Right at the gates of Yellowknife, we settle into a wooded campground sprinkled with large rocks. Behind us, a mountain all our own where we can meditate …

August 5

We dress up to the nines and head over to the Explorer for lunch. It's the largest hotel in Yellowknife and we're guests of Ethel Blondin-Andrew, Secretary of State for Youth. She's accompanied by Glenna Hansen, commissioner for the Territories, i.e., the equivalent of a provincial lieutenant-governor.

Yellowknife, view from The Rock.

A lively and friendly meal, where we discuss politics, Katimavik, the Far North and, especially, the dangers awaiting us if we take the Liard Trail to the Yukon. Over coffee, all we talk about are black bears and grizzlies.

Our two friends insist we participate, this afternoon, in a ceremony and reception in honour of Governor General Adrienne Clarkson, on an official visit of the Territories.

With Ethel Blondin-Andrew, minister responsible for youth, and Glenna Hansen, commissioner for the Territories.

The perfect opportunity to conduct our little propaganda! And to visit the brand new legislative assembly building, where the event is taking place.

Delighted to see Mrs. Clarkson and John Ralston Saul again, this time to talk about Katimavik, which they already think very highly of.

Since not much happens in this lovely little capital of 17,000 people, such a reception brings together the Yellowknife smart set, including the premier, the Honourable Stephen Kakfwi. He's an old friend who would

With Governor General Adrienne Clarkson.

A loyal friend, Stephen Kakfwi, premier of the Northwest Territories

like to see a rapid expansion of Katimavik so that it could return to the Northwest Territories which, unfortunately, were neglected this year, in favour of the Yukon.

They convinced us: we absolutely need a spare tire. It would otherwise be crazy to rush headlong down the bad roads apparently awaiting us over the next days, including the Mackenzie Highway and, especially, the Fort Liard Trail, which isn't very well travelled. Two or three days of gravel roads where you don't see a village for hundreds of kilometres.

We recently discovered that our vehicle doesn't have a spare tire, since the space generally used for this has been filled with water and propane tanks. We're hoping to find a suitable wheel and tire in Yellowknife. We'll have to wait two days to find out: tomorrow is Sunday, and Monday is a holiday.

Following the two hectic weeks we've just had, a two-day break wouldn't be a scandal.

A perfect Sunday at the foot of our "mountain" …

In slow motion, we go about our usual business: I write in my travel log, while Anthony prepares the photos and captions for our next Internet mail out.

I finally get through *Angela's Ashes*, Frank McCourt's wonderful book.

The manager of the campground comes over to ask whether I've seen bears since yesterday. Why, no, I'm sorry! Seems a certain number of them are right inside the campground. Footpaths have been closed and a huge bear trap has been set near our vehicle.

Finally, we're given a list of dos and don'ts to protect ourselves from black bears and grizzlies.

Anthony explores the lake, behind our campsite in Yellowknife.

The first recommendation leaves us baffled: "Avoid camping in areas frequented by bears." Let's say it right out: we have no intention of moving! So, what if we come face to face with a bear on our way to the showers?

"Stop. Stand still. Stay calm." We'll do our best!

"Ensure others know that a bear is in the vicinity." Hence the importance of the cell phone!

"Don't run, shout or make any sudden moves." An attack of generalised paralysis would be dead on!

"Climb at least four metres up a tree to escape a grizzly.

Face to face…

This is ineffective against black bears." What if there are no trees? What if the bear is black?

Then, the ultimate advice, which would make Brigitte Bardot shudder: "If you have a firearm and contact appears unavoidable, shoot to kill!"

August 7

Still on holiday! Everything's closed in town, save for grocery stores, where we'll purchase enough provisions to survive in the desolate back country ahead.

We play tourist. Beer on a terrace overlooking Great Slave Lake. Photo and video from atop The Rock, the town's highest point: a breathtaking view. Lengthy strolls in *old* Yellowknife … whose oldest buildings might date back to 1934, the year the town was founded!

August 8

We leave the campground and its bears before 8:00 a.m. Thanks to a tip from Ethel Blondin-Andrew, we find a used wheel and tire salesman who solves our problem in a flash.

On the road to adventure … according to what we've been told! So-called experts describe a trip on the Mackenzie Highway and, especially, on the Liard Trail as an obstacle course: bumpy roads, potholes, ruts, large rocks. One flat tire after another, etc.

A holiday sky in Yellowknife.

I've often heard similar stories before heading for regions that were even more dangerous: the high plateaus of Ethiopia, the mountains of Afghanistan, the Sahara. I learned to take them with a grain of salt …

Anthony and Jacques in front of the Liard Trail.

The first 200 kilometres to Fort Providence are familiar to us. But, this time, along the Buffalo Park, we see two bison crossing the road, slowly, as though showing us they're at home. Action stations among the videographers. A herd of ten animals follows, then another, and yet another … Okay, that'll do!

Gratefully, we spot a first gas station at the intersection of the Mackenzie Highway and the small road to Fort Providence. Our hopes are dashed: the pump is paralysed by a power failure, and we don't have a clue when it will be fixed. Yet we need fuel and air for the tires …

Rather listlessly, someone suggests we head to Fort Providence itself, a few kilometres to the interior, on the banks of the Mackenzie River. A street lined with sparse houses, a tiny church, a police car, next to nothing. Still, we manage to dig up a very modest gas station which doesn't, however, have an air pump. We'll make do with the air we have!

We head for the next gas station located three hours away. Our trip is now calculated in hours, not kilometres … travelling from one gas station to the next!

Bison, still more bison…

Not a single dwelling. Scrawny evergreens far as the eye can see. Now and again, a cluster of small silver birches bursts into view, as though to dispel the dreary gloom.

Cross Point, at last. A gas pump from another era and a few cabins scattered along a lake of reddish mud.

A twelve-year old boy, probably Inuit, fills our tires with air. He inquires about Katimavik whose name is painted on our truck, intriguing him a little. He should know its meaning: it's the Inuktitut word for "meeting place!"

Anthony hands him a brochure and registration form … He'll be able to complete it in five years!

We leave the Mackenzie Highway, driving onto the Liard Trail we've heard so many bad things about. No lack of pot-holes, but the driving is good. We reach Nahanni National Park around 6:00 p.m. A magnificent campground, of the type we like, in the middle of the forest at the edge of a wild

On the bank of the Mackenzie River.

In Nahanni Park, along the Liard Trail.

lake. We admire the scenery through the bug screen, while having supper mocking the furious mosquito squadrons.

At about 9:00 p.m., while we were already sleeping, the campground warden, a young native in a pickup, arrives in a huff. Very agitated, he asks whether we've heard the honking of a horn in the last minutes. Even the most deafening thunderstorms can't disturb my sleep, but Anthony did hear a few honks … Saying no more, the warden tears off in a cloud of dust and a volley of stones. Another bear story?

A glacial night. No more than 5°C. We turn on the heating system. At ground level, I'm okay. But on the second storey, sheltered from the wind by a mere canvas, Anthony suffers a little from the cold.

At about 7:00 a.m., before leaving this forest crushed beneath the morning silence, we want to question the warden about last night's incident. But his log cabin is padlocked and a sign says: "Open at 9:00 a.m." Too bad! Another bear story (perhaps) whose ending we'll never know.

A strange feeling of solitude. Suddenly, we realize we're probably the only human beings in this stretch of forest.

A footpath in Nahanni Park.

We head off to Fort Liard, over a gravel road pocked with holes and endowed with puddles, reaching the first real mountains since Okotoks in Alberta. We leave the Northwest Territories, making a detour through the northernmost part of British Columbia, before reaching the Yukon.

Between Fort Liard and the Alaska Highway that will take us to Whitehorse lie 175 kilometres of desolation. Not even the shadow of a building. It's raining. A family of resigned buffalo rests in the wet grass by the roadside.

At last, the Alaska Highway, built by American and Canadian soldiers during the war. A land connection was needed in Alaska, in case the Japanese were interested in this far-off American territory.

After about twenty kilometres over this fine paved road, we spot our first black bear, immediately immortalized on video by Anthony.

We reach the northern Rockies, often snow capped even in midsummer.

Towards the Alaska Highway.

A black bear by the roadside.

In the hot and sulfurous waters of the Liard River Hot Springs.

An overnight stop at the Liard River Hot Springs, a British Columbia provincial park. We go over to plunge into a hot spring. A light sulfurous vapour wafts over it. Sheer delight! Paradise! Bliss! We don't speak, allowing ourselves to be intoxicated by the silky murmuring rising from the earth's core.

Return to the campground over a long path lined with ferns and luxuriant plants, exotic flora benefiting from the micro-climate created by the miraculous streaming of the hot springs … 600 kilometres from the Arctic!

Microclimate and exotic flora.

August 10

Departure from Liard River around 8:00 a.m … following another hot bath! This region teams with bears and bison. We see them all along the road, right up to the Yukon border.

Wedged between British Columbia and Alaska, this territory remains an invitation to adventure, to a contemplation of mountains transfixed by quietude, of turbulent rivers

The beauty of Yukon near Whitehorse.

that sparkle as they stream at the bottom of ravines and, now and again, burst into falls, cascades and cataracts.

We drive through Watson Lake, the first small town following the border. A village rather, with a population of barely a thousand souls.

The attraction in Watson Lake: a field haphazardly planted with road signs bearing the names of municipalities in Canada, the United States and elsewhere in the world. Started by a soldier fed up with splitting stones by the Alaska Highway, this strange and useless accumulation boasts 30,000 signs brought by complacent tourists. Even the most absurd collections have a certain power to fascinate ... for the space of an instant!

The large Katimavik house in Whitehorse awaits us with a note pinned to the door, explaining the absence of participants, who are in a debriefing session outside the city: "Make yourselves at home!" Exactly what we'll do, with a completely clear conscience!

August 11

Slept in our little house on wheels, parked beside the large one. Cold night. About 2°C.

I quietly put my notes and accounts in order, while Anthony climbs a mountain with cousins living in the Yukon.

View from a mountain hike, Yukon.

Suddenly, a young man over six-feet tall shows up: "My name is Warren Bradley," he says in French. "I live in Whitehorse, but I've just completed the Katimavik program, which took me to Shelburne, in Nova Scotia, to Shawinigan, in Quebec, and to Vancouver."

Warren relates those seven months of his life with wonderful passion. Ready to do anything to help Katimavik. I'll see him again in three days at the celebration marking the end

Warren Badley, a participant from Whitehorse, has just discovered Nova Scotia, Quebec and Vancouver.

of the program for the area's three groups.

Invited for dinner by the group from the empty house, Anthony and I head over to the Sunshine Valley Guest Ranch, a grand name for a humble cabin where participants are in a debriefing session before their departure. The log cabin is so small that two tents had to be set up to accommodate the group.

Participants went on a long excursion in the mountains, on horseback: following a night in the tent, they barely just

The log cabin where Whitehorse participants hold their last meeting.

got here, exhausted and drenched. But good cheer prevails, and huge steaks are being cooked on the grill, in the open air.

"We rarely eat steak," explains Sarah, the project leader, "but participants did such a good job managing their food budget, that we had a surplus which allowed us to feast tonight."

After dinner, we relax inside the small rustic dwelling, which has neither water nor electricity. A privileged moment, in the glow of a few candles and a small gas lamp.

The actual debriefing then begins. Though we're kindly invited to assist, there's no way we'll impose the presence of strangers on this precious moment in the group's life. After a few minutes, we sneak off and return home: there at least we'll have power and running water!

No water, no electricity.

August 12

We take leave of the participants after breakfast. We'll see them again at Monday's celebration.

Shopping in Whitehorse, then work and read in a park, on the banks of the Yukon River. Nearby, a white mass stands proudly, that of the SS Klondike, a river boat recalling the heroic days of the Gold Rush. People forget that it only lasted five years, at the very end of the 19th century, but had the intensity of a tidal wave. For instance, in 1887, 40,000 prospectors from the south swooped down on the

Yukon, like a plague of locusts. A century later, the entire territory has only 30,000 residents, 23,000 of whom live in Whitehorse.

At 6:30 a.m., an appointment at the other Katimavik house, in the town's centre. Another pleasant meal with participants who are already a little saddened at the prospect of leaving.

August 13

Ken de la Barre invites us for lunch at his place. Another old Katimavik pioneer, he held several important positions with the organization between 1978 and the program's termination. Always filled with original ideas designed to help young people.

At 4:00 p.m., in the basement of the local United Church, we meet the region's three groups, including the one from Atlin, British Columbia, located on the Yukon border. The grand departure for the south is scheduled tomorrow.

Orange and green balloons, the colours of Katimavik, very powerful speakers, good things to eat, and a palpable collective tension, caused by the anguish of impending separation.

The customary speech. The mayor's representative urges us to return to the Yukon next year, while—he already knows it!—that won't be possible without a budget increase.

A few participants were designated by their peers to speak in everyone's name. Among the most touching ones: Nick Oliver from Saint Mary's, Ontario. Trying to explain everything the program has brought him and all the gratitude he feels towards the people of Whitehorse, he can hardly contain his emotions.

Yet even more moving is the testimony from Ashley Rideout, a participant from Pasadena, Newfoundland, over there, at the other end ... She bursts into tears with each phrase. At the end, she bawls her eyes out, while a huge

Ashley Rideout from Newfoundland thanks Whitehorse. She bursts into tears...

Nick tries to console her, wrapping his long awkward arms around her.

The entire hall is overcome by emotion, people are hugging, clutching very tightly in clusters of three or four ... You could fill a lake with all the wonderful tears shed by Katimavik participants since 1977 ...

To ensure the evening doesn't turn into a melodrama, the emcee, a participant from Montreal, Young-mi Lee, grabs the microphone: "And now," she says energetically, "let the

Emotions on the eve of departure.

party begin!" The loudspeakers immediately pour out a deluge of decibels, as everyone starts dancing.

Once again, Anthony and I slip away before the end to resume our journey. Very important not to miss the British Columbia groups, whose program is also drawing to a close!

We have to be in Prince Rupert in 48 hours! We therefore leave Whitehorse around 7:00 p.m. with the intention of camping at the farthest possible site, near Teslin, along the Alaska Highway. We're in luck: daylight lasts till 11:00 p.m…

Chapter 8

BEETHOVEN IN THE ROCKIES

British Columbia

August 14

We were told the Stewart-Cassiar Road is a nightmare: we'll therefore rise at 5:30 a.m., with the first glimmer of dawn.

Back on the southbound road.

Two hours later, we fill up at the intersection of the Alaska Highway and the Stewart-Cassiar Road, which looks much like a country road, at times paved, at times gravel, always under construction, crammed with hills and curves.

But the scenery is spectacular and wild, lined with restive tall conifers, like a legion of delirious Don Quixote's. A shower of tiny lakes sparkle amid a sea of greenery, raging rivers, likely seething with salmon, endless stretches of wildflowers, at times dark violet like the night, at times burnt orange, at times golden like the corn mustard. And all round, the high coastal mountains whose peaks are capped with snow in mid-August.

On the Stewart-Cassiar Road.

Towns grow scarce, tiny hamlets, clusters of three or four cabins. A gas station every 250 kilometres.

During his endless hours at the wheel, Anthony often listens to music, as though to be more alert. He has his CDs, I have mine.

Though we've found several points in common, our musical tastes are clearly poles apart or nearly ... In this regard, there may be a fifty-year difference between us!

A valley in northern British Columbia.

Since Anthony needs his music to drive, I put up with it willingly, but can't manage to get used to the monotone techno, whose nervous, aggressive and metallic rhythm reminds me of some broken-down machine in the midst of delirium.

One day, I asserted myself by slipping a Mozart sonata and a Beethoven concerto into our CD player. I asked Anthony if he liked the music:

"Yes, of course!" he answered without hesitation. But never afterwards did he ask to hear another classical CD!

We were better able to reach a compromise in the area of popular songs. I very quickly flipped for Caetano Veloso, the big Brazilian star. For his part, Anthony admits I got him to like Léo Ferré, and some songs by Trenet.

Following eleven hours on the road, Bell II, a small town. A campground without trimmings, but with a shower.

August 15

Quite exceptionally we rise at 9:00 a.m., since we're now sure of reaching Terrace well ahead of schedule.

As we drive farther south and closer to the Pacific coast, the countryside changes profoundly (as do participants!). Deciduous trees crop up in wild strips, crowding out the rugged uniformity of coniferous forests.

In Terrace, a small town of 13,000 inhabitants which clings to the banks of the Skeena River, we meet with Nathan Rowlen, the regional coordinator. We follow him down a narrow road leading to a nearby lake. Terrace participants

The group's cottage in Terrace, B.C.

are here, having almost completed their debriefing inside a very rudimentary cottage: neither running water nor electricity. It's an obsession!

No lack of electricity in the air, however. Following seven months of intense living, of conflicts always solved in the end, of heartrending ordeals, like the departure of a group member, of hard monotonous work, now a source of pride,

With Terrace participants.

following this unique experience, the moment has come when everyone will go off in their own direction, trying to pick up a "normal" life with parents, friends and the school they knew seven months ago, considerably different from the School of Life ...

Yes, there's electricity in the air, a hint of anguish as well before this return to the past, to the unknown in fact, since each participant feels totally different from what they were *before*. I'm remindedof an expression by San Antonio: "He's changed so much that he had trouble recognizing me!"

Participants tease each other, pretend to argue, hazard furtive caresses that say a lot about the tender friendship that now unites these boys and girls "forever," as they say. Last night, confides one of the girls in the group, the cup spilled over and tears flowed warmly and profusely, before vanishing into volleys of laughter.

Anthony and I temper outbursts somewhatby our presence, as does the arrival of guests to this evening's celebration, our friends from Terrace. Host families, community partners show up with huge salads, plates of cookies, cakes. A mother even has her newborn in her arms. "He's my little brother!" exclaims a huge participant. He grabs the baby, cuddles, kisses and nibbles at it, as though it really were his little brother. A guy from Sherbrooke, Quebec, who's leaving tomorrow morning ...

A wonderful fraternal pleasant evening, illuminated by oil lamps and daylight drowning endlessly in the beautiful lake of purple ink.

Knowing full well participants will stretch this final night to the limit, Anthony and I leave at about 10:00 p.m.

End of the dream...

August 16

At 7:30 a.m., even those who talked till 3:00 a.m. are beginning to pile their luggage into the Katimavik van, parked beside ours.

We get up to make our farewells and for the privilege of witnessing this intense and feverish moment, where a group climbs into the white van for the last time, knowing the next stop is the bus station or the airport, which is to say, the end of the joy.

Along the Skeena River, heading to Prince Rupert, B.C.

According to *National Geographic Magazine*, the road linking us to Prince Rupert is among the ten most spectacular in the world. What luck to quietly discover it, at first beneath a gentle rain, so typical of this region that a sparkling sun would seem out of place. We follow the Skeena River's voluptuous curves to our left and, to the right, a long procession of puffy clouds colliding with the mountains.

In Prince Rupert, we meet the last two participants on our list, the others having left the city yesterday. For their part, Pierre-Luc Michaud from Amos and Audrey Turner from Charlesbourg have decided to take the long way home to Quebec, i.e., the train. Thanks to Katimavik, they were able to discover Ontario, British Columbia, and even a corner of Quebec they didn't know. But they want to see more. They've missed seeing wide stretches of the Rockies, the jewels of Banff and Jasper, the three Prairie Provinces …

Pierre-Luc Michaud from Amos, Quebec, at the time of departure from Prince Rupert: "I changed a great deal!"

We chat at leisure inside a small Prince Rupert café, whose lentil soup is worth the detour. For nearly two hours, there's so much to say. The experiences of Pierre-Luc and Audrey don't differ much from those of the hundreds of participants we met since leaving Newfoundland. But for every one of them, each effort, ordeal and victory is a unique moment that will mark their lives. They know it very well. We know it too, and that's why we listen to their confidences as though we'd never heard similar ones.

"I changed a great deal!" Audrey declares.

Audrey Turner from Charlesbourg, Quebec: "I changed a great deal!"

"I changed a great deal!" says Pierre-Luc in turn, like an emotional echo.

"Learning to work, to communicate in two languages, to live in a group for seven months, survive ordeals, share profound joys, discover this huge country … " says Audrey, unless it was Pierre-Luc. Anyhow, they always agree!

On taking leave of these two beautiful participants, Anthony and I have the impression, as well, that a moment in our lives is drawing to a close, that we'll soon return home, different from what we were before departing. In a few weeks …

At Campbell River, on Vancouver Island, we'll drop in on a group of project leaders at their training camp. We feel a strong urge to take the ferry from Prince Albert to Port Hardy, at the northern tip of the island. Not very expensive, since we avoid 2,000 kilometres of mountainous roads …

Everyone tells us the ocean trip's worth it. For some fifteen hours the ship weaves through the wild islands of the Inside Passage. Something that should allow us to rest. Especially Anthony, who's shackled to the steering wheel for days on end.

But we're on a waiting list. It's high season and our chances of finding a spot aboard the ferry are rather slim. We spend the night at a campground near the landing pier. Full of hope …

August 17

Up at 5:00 a.m. No slacking! We want to head the lineup of cars that will agonize through the night until told to board. By the time our turn arrived, we'd almost given up ...

Among the wild islands of the Inside Passage.

Our distress is quickly rewarded by the dazzling scenery we gently glide through, effortlessly, happy as kings. Alas, a light rain, a mist really, discourages lengthy strolls on deck.

The ship is filled with German tourists travelling in clusters, as though crowded inside an invisible bubble. "Whale to port!" blare the loudspeakers. And the bubble rolls to port. The cafeteria has made provisions for sauerkraut ...

At day's end, the sun manages to break through the last nimbus and to set magnificently, showering the mountainous islands with specks of gold … Engleman spruces, balsam and Douglas firs storm up the mountains, the highest reaching a thousand metres.

"Whale to port!"

We dock in Port Hardy a little before midnight: the first campground will do. We're in luck: a forest of tall cedars, like clumsy blind giants shoving each other in the murk. The impression of entering the deep night of a gothic cathedral planted with enormous black columns.

The sun returns to enchant the Inside Passage.

Time to get up in Port Hardy, B.C., amid giant evergreens.

At the training camp in Campbell River, BC.

August 18

Everything's changed by the time we awaken. The miracle of light has placed us amid amazing splendour, a festival of nature, in praise of our country's most beautiful conifers. They're still dripping with the taunting rain that tickles the rustling ferns.

Although a mere drizzle, the rain prevents a full view of the mountain display surrounding us: their dark mass is silhouetted against an iron-gray sky or fades behind a veil of clouds. Video alert: a doe and her fawn are gambolling by the roadside.

In Campbell River, the Katimavik house from which a last group has just, alas, departed. Before another occupies it in September, it's being used as a training camp for the region's future project leaders, under Adam Wood's very competent management. A word of welcome pinned to the door, along with an admirable quote from Gandhi, which could be Katimavik's motto: "You must be the change you wish to see in the world."

Lengthy discussions with these young people, some of them project leaders with a good deal of experience. We assess the effects of budget cuts on the program's quality; for instance, the necessity of holding five small regional training camps, like this one, instead of a single larger one, at the centre of the country, where the richness of the group was multiplied fivefold.

First glimpses of the Pacific.

August 19

A follow-up to our discussions with those who will be project leaders in the autumn and who'll play a major role in the life of their groups and in the development of participants.

Back on the road, southbound, a little after noon. Near Fort Alberni, the tallest trees seen in our lives. Some tall as forty-five storey buildings, and many over eight-hundred years old. Driving along the Pacific, an eternity of wavelets gleaming with the splendour of day's end.

Night in the Pacific Rim campground.

On Vancouver Island, the huge trees of Cathedral Grove.

August 20

Brief stop in Tofino, a surfing centre and hot spot of bourgeois tourism in the region. A little too fancy for us!

We again drive through the mountain range splitting Vancouver Island in two, like a conceited spinal chord. A corkscrew road winds its way through as best it can.

Stop for the rest of the day at Qualium Falls Provincial Park. Anthony has an appointment here with one of his former participants from the area. Around 5:30 p.m., a tall

Brenden Galloway, one of Anthony's former participants, in Qualicum Falls, B.C.

fellow with a blonde mane drops in. Brenden Galloway. Always impressive to observe bonds created between participants and project leaders. They trade stories, I fix the meal.

August 21

We'd expected to spend a quiet day in this ferocious park, comfort-bereft but planted with giant conifers seen nowhere else in Canada. A phone call changes our plans. Katimavik Executive Director Jean-Guy Bigeau wants Anthony to show a mini video of our trip at a reception scheduled to celebrate our return in September.

A dreamy corner of Vancouver Island.

This will require a few days' work and, particularly for our videographer, an editing studio, easier to find in Vancouver than in this park. We therefore give up our day in the forest, quickly hopping the ferry linking Nanaimo to the mainland.

Since Katimavik's regional office is in Burnaby, a district municipality of Greater Vancouver, we drop anchor there. At a campground of the commercial type, the likes of which we'd shunned like the plague to this day. Trees are scarce, recreational vehicles are planted in straight lines, barely separated by shrub hedges. But it's a stone's toss from Burnaby and the showers are splendid!

August 22

Anthony abandons me to my fate, becoming a full-time videographer. Since he'll stay with friends, I'll see him again in a few days.

At the regional office, I meet Jackie Neal, the brand new regional director for British Columbia and Yukon, and Gordon Thériault, who once filled that job, from the beginning to the dark years when the program was cancelled. In 1994, soon as the flame had been rekindled, he returned to the Katimavik fold as a board member. We talk about meetings scheduled for the next four days, mainly with the media.

August 25

A quiet and solitary day in this huge campground designed for recreational vehicles, as they call them, from the most modest (like ours!) to the longest plumpest trailers.

I head to downtown Vancouver to do an interview on the Terry Moore show, an apparently very popular radio program. I insist that a participant, either boy or girl, accompany me. The regional office designates Joel Lindsay, a remarkable young man. Previously shy, he admits on air that this is his first radio experience: "Without having just gone through the Katimavik program, I'd have never had the courage to show up here!"

Questions from the audience follow the interview. Many give moving testimonies, including a few participants from way back, who've maintained a keen interest even after twenty years ... A single discordant note: a Vancouver man finds the program excellent, but a little costly ... at

$125,000 a participant. He's added at least one zero too many and I kindly send him back to his calculator!

August 28

Anthony returns. He isn't very pleased with the ten-minute video produced in a hurry but, when we get back, he'll take the time to produce an everlasting masterpiece!

The beautiful Osoyoos Valley, B.C.

We finally set out for the Rockies, where we'll live till we reach Alberta.

August 29

According to the account of his trip to Canada,[7] Maurice Genevoix had exclaimed: "The Rockies, the most beautiful scenery our world can offer!" How right he is. And it's impossible to weary of these high places, invigorating to the body, stirring to the soul.

The little dirt road to Gibson Lake, B.C.

We camp in Kokanee Park, where the highest peaks, we're told, rise to 3,424 metres.

We aren't very far from Kokanee Lake, where Michel, Pierre Trudeau's youngest son, met a tragic end in November 1998. He still rests at the bottom of the lake, surrounded by tall steep mountains, a spectacular sepulchre for a young sportsman filled with ideals.

This tragedy had deeply shaken Pierre Trudeau, who never got over his sorrow, as his friends can attest.

The proximity of Kokanee Lake prods me to go and see it, without anyone knowing, since I've nothing but contempt for those who exploit Trudeau's name. Anthony and I agree this detour will be mentioned neither in my account nor in his video. A strictly personal visit I intended mentioning to no one, not even Michel's father.

August 30

We take the lousy little dirt road leading to Gibson Lake, where the drive ends and the trail begins.

For a long half hour we're jolted, jiggled, shaken like rag dolls, springs creaking and coachwork twisting. Anthony works wonders to avoid branches, potholes, precipices.

The surrounding scenery changes from one minute to the next, with each turn, at the top of each hill. An endless succession of trees caress cloud after cloud. Mountains with bare slopes, and sharp snow-white ridges, unexpected vegetation recalling the Alps.

We finally reach Gibson Lake and a clearing where vehicles can be parked: the end of the road. From here on, we walk!

The makeshift parking lot is unsupervised, but billboards covered in notices, advice and warnings portend the wild country, where animals are more at home than humans. For example, a sign entreats us to wrap the vehicle's wheels with chicken wire: porcupines around here like to nibble on tires! Luckily, some traveller left behind his wire-mesh armour. Likely to make it available to innocents of our ilk, more wary of grizzlies than porcupines.

We're also warned about bears, and advised to shake a bell while walking to keep them away. In Whitehorse, I'd purchased a bear-bell for my granddaughter, Jeanne, to whom I'd soon relate my bear stories. I never imagined it would come in handy some day, along this remote trail … which I take with some apprehension unrelated to the bears: despite my boasting, I realize I'm in my seventies, and less able than I was at twenty to make such climbs.

A trail linking Gibson Lake to Kokanee Lake.

With the charming sound of the hand-bell dangling from Anthony's pack, we decidedly embark on what may be the world's most spectacular trail. Signs tell us a two-and-a-quarter hour hike will take us from Gibson Lake to Kokanee Lake.

We climb, nearly always climb, at times clutching branches wherever the slope is too steep. I wheeze like a pair of old bagpipes while Anthony scampers along, hopping left and right, to photograph a flower, a snow-clad peak, or an overly curious tiny rodent.

*The most
beautiful trail in
the world …
Perhaps!*

I stop frequently: "Look at the amazing scenery, Anthony!" In fact, I need to catch my breath more often than he does … Sometimes wondering if I'll have strength to make it.

At last, following a steep and treacherous slope, the reward: a beautiful round mirror, whose smooth and icy waters reflect the bare slopes of the mountain which rises before us like a wall. At the very top, Kokanee Glacier, birthplace of the avalanche that swept Michel Trudeau into the lake to his death.

Seated on a boulder, I contemplate the smooth surface of the lake and its unfathomable depths. And think of Michel, whom I knew so little. I first saw him as an adorable baby in his mother's arms, then as a happy child hopping around the rooms at 24 Sussex in his pyjamas, in a bathing suit on a Jamaicam beach, as a dreamy teenager looking at his father with love and admiration … And it's through his father's eyes that I afterwards saw him grow up from afar.

We sometimes feel we're in the Alps…

When we lunched together, at some point I'd ask: "And how are the boys?" With patent delight, he'd proceed to inform me that Justin was teaching somewhere in British Columbia, Sacha was shooting a documentary in some war-torn African country, and that Michel was skiing and giving lessons in the Rockies, where his father always dreamed of soon joining him on the most redoubtable slopes.

Seated on my boulder, I think of Michel, but also, especially, of his father, my friend, so struck down by his son's death that something snapped inside him, as though forever.

*After more than
two hours
climbing ... our
reward.*

Silently, we walk back to the trailhead. The descent is nearly as difficult as the climb, especially since my leg muscles,
not used to this kind of exertion, are beginning to protest.
I lose my footing on a very steep slope covered in tiny peb-
bles, pretty nearly tumbling into a ravine.

Back on the highway, heading to Nakusp where there's a
campground near a spring of hot mineralised water: the
ultimate luxury and supreme remedy to soothe my aching
muscles and warm my old bones ... A persistent vapour
reminds us the water is very hot. A sign indicates 104⁰ F ...
and forbids us to stay more than twenty minutes, though
we dream of letting it lull us for hours, days, till the end of
time ...

A beautiful round mirror: Kokanee Lake.

August 31

Bravely, we rise at 6:00 a.m. to take advantage of the longest day possible through the "traditional" Rockies of the national park leading to Banff, Alberta.

We drive along huge lakes, awash with light, the Columbia River, proud and magnificent. And all round, the tallest mountains in the country.

I treat myself to something I'd long dreamed of: crossing the Rockies listening to Beethoven's Ninth Symphony, with the Ode to Joy bursting amid the snowy peaks.

Even Anthony agrees it's a good idea ...

Chapter 9

A HASTY RETURN

Alberta, Saskatchewan, Manitoba,
Ontario, Quebec

August 31

We stop at Lake Louise, a thousandfold less beautiful than Kokanee Lake, overrun by tourists from all over the country and every continent, swamped with distraught Japanese who seem to have lost their guide.

Inescapable Lake Louise.

A stroll through Banff's lovely streets right up to the Banff Centre for the Arts, where I once stayed briefly and where Anthony dreams of going to perfect his art.

By the end of that memorable day, Calgary, and a camp-ground 35 kilometres from the city.

At night, an impressive display created by Calgary's lights, like a field of yellow stars.

Calgary by night, seen from the campground.

September 2

I meet up with my eldest son, Michel, who adores Calgary, where he's lived for twenty years. In his incredible 1968 convertible Impala, he gives us a tour of the town which he knows like the back of his hand, briskly helping us with our errands.

The three of us repair to a very "in" restaurant, i.e., one where the amplifier is so powerful that it prevents any conversation. We have a delightful time nonetheless ...

On the road to Medicine Hat ... whose strange name has always intrigued me. So let's settle the question once and for all: it's a translation of the Indian word *saamis*, which means "the medicine man's hat." Following a battle between the Cree and Blackfoot, the Cree shaman took flight, losing his hat in the middle of the Alberta River. Convinced this was a bad omen, the Cree laid down their

The incredible 1968 Impala convertible...

The wonderful tranquillity of the provincial park.

Towards the campground in Cypress Hills, Alberta.

weapons and were quickly slaughtered by the fearless Blackfoot. And there you have it!

We end up in an Alberta provincial park which straddles the Saskatchewan border.

It's late in the season, and campers are growing more scarce. Wonderful impression of being alone before a lovely lake, in which a phantasmagorical sunset drowns itself, something these flat provinces have a knack for. during the night, a concert of howling coyotes reminds we aren't really alone in the world …

September 3

Driving towards Regina on a staggering four-lane highway, unchanging, rectilinear, as though drawn with a ruler. After a month in mountain country, we fear the monotony of these enormous freshly harvested fields. But, on the contrary, we're delighted to be back on the infinite plain, soothing, forever changing.

A few hours in Regina, then back on the straight road, without the least hint of a curve. Night at a provincial park near Qu'Appelle, another strange name ... which, to me, will remain a mystery for a while still! A lovely wood of conifer rows, obviously imported and planted.

As we stroll about, we meet a few families with children and, especially, oldish people of independent means, who've invested their savings in potbellied recreational vehicles, some large as Greyhound buses.

The prairie, an incredible rectilinear road ...

They're enlarged even more with endless awnings under which imposing lawn furniture is scattered. Amid all this plastic, a huge TV sits enthroned complete with the requisite satellite dish.

Adding a little to the atmosphere, some people even hang electrical lanterns from branches, which then start to look like Christmas trees. People drop by from one vehicle to the next, trade RV stories, congratulate each other on the latest gadgets added to all the others, and make plans to meet at the next campground ... in two days or next summer! A peculiar world we observe from afar with discrete and somewhat detached curiosity.

September 4

To avoid retracing our path, we'll drive to Winnipeg along a secondary road, which gives an idea of the incredible isolation of western farmers. Kilometres of fields separate neighbours from each other. Practically no cars on the road, fewer pedestrians still. Near Melville, a slender and terrified stag skips across the road, like a huge grasshopper: he didn't expect to see people!

Winnipeg, still dozing at the end of the long labour day weekend. Streets deserted, stores closed. We dash off to Birds Hill Provincial Park. Its campground is very well layed out, vast and sufficiently wooded to prevent us from seeing other campers. Our only visitors: jackrabbits!

September 5

Dinner and evening with Sharon Carstairs and her husband John. They live in a lovely wooden house at the edge of Lake Winnipeg, where we spend delightful hours in the warmth of friendship.

An educator at heart, Senator Carstairs has always shown very sincere interest in Katimavik, to the point she's never turned down an opportunity to meet groups of participants. She understands the program's objectives, and has often championed it before her Senate and Commons' colleagues. A precious ally with whom it's a complete delight talking about Katimavik and it's future.

Near Lake Winnipeg with Sharon and John Carstairs.

September 7

Before leaving Winnipeg, a press conference in one of the city's restaurants. Everything goes smoothly till one of the reporters informs us, as well as his colleagues who are still there, of the news deeply distressing all of Canada. He's just heard on the radio that Pierre Trudeau's very sick, perhaps at death's door.

Many of the journalists had already left, but those remaining pester me with questions about the former prime minister, arguing that we're old friends. But I only know what I've just heard, and really don't want to speculate on the subject. As best I can, without offending anyone, I manage to pull myself out of this hornet's nest.

We quickly jump into the van and drive off. The cell phone rings nonstop: I decline at least twenty interviews concerning Pierre Trudeau. Interest is so keen that journalists have completely forgotten the purpose of our trip … no longer wanting to hear a thing about it!

A little before reaching Kenora, we spot people in the middle of the road waving at us to stop. A television crew, determined to interview me at any cost. Their camera is already set up on the roadside. Following discussions, we agree on doing two interviews: one about Trudeau, the other about Katimavik.

Resuming our journey, we conclude it will now be impossible to draw the media's attention to Katimavik. Journalists have only one thing in mind: wresting a few words from me about my friend, for the six o'clock news!

We therefore decide to take the shortest route back to Montreal, bypassing even Toronto. In any event, our mission was drawing to a close, and if speculation about Pierre Trudeau's illness is the slightest bit right, I don't want to waste another minute, in the hope of seeing him one last time.

A television crew awaits us in the middle of the road.

Since the death of Michel, and especially since last year, I'd observed my friend's health slipping, but was far from suspecting it would deteriorate so fast. A few weeks, perhaps a month ago, I'd spoken to him over the cell phone. We'd joked as usual, he'd even traded a few words with Anthony. Before leaving him I'd said half-heartedly: "I see the summer's done you wonders. Your voice sounds good … You're getting better!"

Following a few seconds of silence, he answered, serenely but firmly: "No, Jacques, I'm not getting better."

We take short cuts on the road to Thunder Bay, finally stopping in Dryden for the night.

The lovely scenery of northern Ontario.

September 8

Today, we set a trip record: 1,100 kilometres, most of them with Anthony driving.

We camp outside Sault-Sainte-Marie, at the edge of Georgian Bay, set ablaze by a glowing sunset.

Without being certain, we're hopeful of reaching Montreal tomorrow night. So this could be the last dinner of our trip. We therefore improvise a little feast, beginning with the traditional avocado with olive oil and lemon, but this time the Neapolitan spaghetti is washed down with a little Bordeaux which had bided its time at the back of the cupboard.

With help from the wine, we have the impression of being old friends.

A drink to our success … We're finally reaching the end of this long voyage, having overcome our minor differences and making, all things considered, a remarkable team.

A last supper of avocados with olive oil and lemon…

But the adventure doesn't stop here, since Anthony will have to produce a video, and I'll arrange my travel notes into a little book, abundantly illustrated with his photos. So we haven't finished working together.

My travelling companion doesn't readily show his emotions. While I'm an extrovert, no doubt atrocious, Anthony remains more reserved; I have the impression I've barely scratched the surface with him.

But this evening, with help from a little wine, we get the feeling we're old friends …

September 9

Up at 5:30 a.m. Without beating yesterday's record, we drive nearly nonstop the thousand or so kilometres between Sault-Sainte-Marie and Montreal. I've no recollection of this endless journey: it's a truism that 24 hours before the end of a long trip, you've already reached your destination. The tired horse nearing the stable only dreams of fresh water and dry hay scented with clover.

The sun rises over the journey one last time.

EPILOGUE

Ordinary folks can have the most fantabulous ideas, the most crazy wonderful dreams: as a rule, nothing happens unless they can share them with a prince who's sensitive to the fantabulous and wonderful, who's able to make dreams come true.

I was an ordinary guy and had the unique opportunity of knowing Pierre Trudeau in our youths and to have kept his trust and friendship. When he became prime minister, he didn't always agree with my grand schemes, and God knows he dismissed several!

However, he was immediately passionate about Canada World Youth and, a few years later, about Katimavik, whose enormous possibilities he grasped, among others that of changing our society completely.

Without Pierre Trudeau, neither Canada World Youth, nor Katimavik, would've seen the day. And till his death, we never met without his speaking fondly of one or the other. As well, he'd shown a lot of enthusiasm when I mentioned my plans for this trip. We agreed I'd tell him all about it on my return, at our usual Chinese restaurant, the Chrysanthème. I was far from suspecting that, for the two of us, there'd be no more Chrysanthème …

On reaching Montreal, I get in touch with Sacha: he confirms his father's in a very bad way. Bed-ridden for the last several days, seeing only members of his family. I understand.

Next day, Sacha calls back: "My father says he wants to see you. Try to come over around 4:00 p.m., the only time of day we have him sit in a chair for an hour or so ... "

This great sportsman, so proud of his physical fitness, is now but the shadow of himself: a frail old man for whom even the slightest word requires incredible effort.

So I talk, talk, relate, relate, without too much knowing what I'm saying. At times, an anecdote wrests a faint smile from him ... When I quote the touching words of a Katimavik participant, whose "life will never again be the same," his noble face lights up ... When I broach the Rockies, I realize the memory of Michel has swept through his soul.

Oh! and I'd promised myself to speak to no one of my excursion to Kokanee Lake, not even to my friend. But, at this moment, I know I won't see him again. And what if an allusion to that very simple gesture of friendship provides him with a small joy?

"And then we went all the way up to Kokanee Lake ... "

His exhausted eyes light up before slightly misting over. With great effort, he asks me in a nearly inaudible voice: "On foot? ... On foot?" He knows the area, the steep winding trail ... He has trouble believing I managed to hike up to the lake! He's delighted. I'm delighted.

By making Katimavik possible—there were 5,000 participants in the last year of his government and, together, we'd
dreamed of 50,000 or more!—Pierre Trudeau was leaving
way more than a monument to the youth of his country: he
was giving them an effective means for taking charge of
their lives, surpassing themselves, becoming citizens open
to the world, free men and women. He was bequeathing
what has rightly been called the School of Life!

APPENDICES

A – Mission and Objectives

Mission

Katimavik, Canada's national youth corps, has given itself the mission to **foster the personal development of our nation's young people** through a challenging program of volunteer community work, training and group interaction.

Objectives

1. To contribute substantially to the personal, social and professional development of participants.

2. To promote community service.

3. To offer a diversified experience fostering a better understanding of the Canadian reality.

B – *Katimavik Program*

Katimavik offers young Canadians aged 17 to 21 an opportunity, free of charge, to acquire interpersonal and work skills, while learning a second language.

For seven months, Katimavik participants live in three regions of Canada (one of which is French-speaking) as a member of a group of eleven (including a Project Leader who supervises the learning experience) comprising an equal number of young men and women from all parts of Canada. Participants, who are selected to reflect Canada's cultural, economic and social diversity, also spend nine days in each region living with a host family, to better understand the local culture.

Participants work as volunteers on community projects, while immersing themselves in the social and cultural activities of their three host communities. Work projects and group living help participants become aware of their potential and the requirements of the labour market.

At the same time, to achieve the program's learning objectives, participants organize a series of activities outside their working hours in five areas: second language, leadership, environment, culture and lifestyle.

Katimavik is an experience whose intensity nurtures openness and maturity in its young participants at a turning point in their lives. Many parents of participants say that Katimavik was an experience that helped their children make enlightened decisions about their future.

C – Application Form

I WANT TO APPLY!

Fill out and return to (PLEASE PRINT):

> Katimavik
> Port of Montreal Building, Wing 3, Suite 2160
> Cité du Havre
> Montreal, Quebec, H3C 3R5
> Telephone (toll-free): 1-888 525-1503
> Fax: (514) 868-0901
> E-mail: info@katimavik.org

LAST NAME(S)   FIRST NAME

ADDRESS (INCLUDING APARTMENT NUMBER)   CITY

PROVINCE   POSTAL CODE   E-MAIL ADDRESS

TELEPHONE NUMBER   FAX NUMBER

LANGUAGE OF CORRESPONDENCE   SEX   DATE OF BIRTH

The following information is requested for statistical purposes:

Where did you hear about Katimavik?

What is your current status?

❑ student   ❑ employed   ❑ unemployed

What is your annual family income?

Are you an Aboriginal person?

An Aboriginal person is a North American Indian or a member of a First Nation, a Métis, or Inuit. North American Indians or members of a First Nation include status, treaty or registered Indians, as well as non-status and non-registered Indians.

❏ No

❏ Yes (please check the appropriate box)

    ❏ Inuit ❏ Métis
    ❏ North American Indian / First Nation

Are you a member of a visible minority?

❏ No

❏ Yes (please check the box that best describes the group to which you belong)

    ❏ Black ❏ Non-white Latin American (including indigenous persons from Central and South America, etc.)
    ❏ Persons of Mixed Origin (with one parent in one of the visible minority groups listed here)
    ❏ Chinese ❏ Japanese ❏ Korean ❏ Filipino
    ❏ South Asian / East Indian (Indian from India; Bangladeshi; Pakistani; East Indian from Guyana, Trinidad, East Africa; etc.)
    ❏ Non-white West Asian, North African or Arab (including Egyptian; Libyan; Lebanese; Iranian; etc.)
    ❏ Southeast Asian (including Burmese; Cambodian; Laotian; Thai; Vietnamese; etc.)
    ❏ Other visible minority (please specify):
_____

www.katimavik.org

The Government of Canada, through Exchanges Canada, a part of the Department of Canadian Heritage, is proud to provide financial assistance to Katimavik.

D – Katimavik Offices

HEAD OFFICE

Port of Montreal Building
Wing 3, Suite 2160, Cité du Havre
Montreal, Quebec H3C 3R5
Phone: 1-888-525-1503
        (514) 868-0898
Fax: (514) 868-0901
E-mail: info@katimavik.org

REGIONAL OFFICES

BRITISH COLUMBIA AND YUKON
    Unit # 1, 774 Columbia St.
    New Westminster, British Columbia
    V3M 1B5
    Phone: (604) 521-0555
    Fax: (604) 521-9393

PRAIRIES, NORTHWEST TERRITORIES AND NUNAVUT
    827-601 Spadina Cres. East
    Saskatoon, Saskatchewan
    S7K 3G8
    Phone: (306) 665-2122
    Fax: (306) 665-0211

ONTARIO
    298 Elgin Street, Suite 101
    Ottawa, Ontario
    K2P 1M3
    Phone: (613) 722-8091
    Fax: (613) 722-1359

QUEBEC

Port of Montreal Building
Wing 3, Suite 2160
Cité du Havre
Montreal, Québec
H3C 3R5
Phone: (514) 871-2043
Fax: (514) 871-8518

ATLANTIC

35 Highfield Street, Suite 3
Moncton, New Brunswick
E1C 5N1
Phone: (506) 859-4353
Fax: (506) 859-4322

E – Board of Directors 2001

Founding President
Jacques HÉBERT*
Montreal, Québec

Life Member
Claude RAÎCHE
Notre-Dame-de-l'Île-Perrot, Québec

Co-Chair
Sylvie C. CREVIER*
Management Consultant
Les Cèdres, Quebec

Co-Chair
Max BECK*
Consultant, businessman
Toronto, Ontario

Vice-Chair
Gordon THÉRRIAULT*
Executive Director
Big Brothers of Greater Vancouver
Vancouver, British Columbia

Secretary
André DUFOUR*
Borden Ladner Gervais
Montreal, Quebec

Treasurer
Michael D. SMITH*
Programmer - 3D Modelling
Softimage
Montreal, Quebec

Members

Kell ANTOFT
Atlantic region

Richard GERVAIS
Quebec region

Jim COUTTS
Ontario region

Bruce GILBERT
Atlantic region

Theresa HOHNE
British Columbia/Yukon region

Huguette LABELLE
Ontario region

Sherry PEDEN
Prairies region

Susan VEIT
British Columbia/Yukon region

Ex officio Member
Jean-Guy BIGEAU*
Executive Director
KATIMAVIK
Montreal, Quebec

---

*   *The asterisk indicates that the person is also a member of the Executive Committee.*